The Thinking That Feels

International Studies in Law and Literature

Editor-in-Chief

VOLUME 5

The titles published in this series are listed at *brill.com/isll*

The Thinking That Feels

Practices in Law and Humanities

By

M. Paola Mittica

Translated from the Italian by

Mark Byrne

BRILL | NIJHOFF

This work was originally published by G. Giappichelli editore in 2022 under the title *Il pensiero che sente. Pratiche di Law and Humanities.*

ISSN 2773–191X
ISBN 978-90-04-75770-7
ISBN 978-90-04-75771-4 (PDF)
DOI https://doi.org/10.1163/9789004757714

Library of Congress Control Number: 2026906818

Brill Nijhoff and Koninklijke Brill BV are part of De Gruyter Brill.
www.degruyterbrill.com

Questions about General Product Safety Regulation: productsafety@degruyterbrill.com

Given the spectacle of their teeming successes, the nations of the West had no trouble exalting history, attributing to it a meaning and a finality. It belonged to them; they were its agents: hence, it must take a rational course. Consequently, they placed it under the patronage, by turns, of Providence, of Reason, and of Progress. What they lacked was a sense of fatality, which they are at last beginning to acquire, overwhelmed by the absence which lies in wait for them, by the prospect of their eclipse. Once subjects, they have become objects, forever dispossessed of that luminescence, that admirable megalomania which had hitherto protected them from the irreparable.

Cioran 1968, 48–49

Contents

Foreword

It is not the number of pages that determines the quality of a book; there are brief, intense works that leave behind a deep and lasting impression. The book by Paola Mittica that you are about to read is one of these. It develops a demanding thesis within its radical simplicity: a true understanding of law – as well as its just practice – requires a form of thought that is also sensitive. Sensitive in the double sense of mobilizing sensations and feelings, and thus the body and our affective capacities.

Thus "provoked" (that is, questioned, called into being – from *provocare*), law is considered not only in its most familiar surface aspect – a system of axioms and concepts, of codified norms, procedural structures, and institutional frameworks – but also, and above all, in its submerged depth: the anthropological and social environment within which it develops and outside of which we perceive only its empty forms. Something like the *nomos* of which Robert Cover spoke: the normative world we inhabit, woven from evaluations, narratives, images, values, and norms – a world to which sensibility offers privileged access.

The turn toward the social sciences undertaken in legal studies a few decades ago, with its renewed interest in "interdisciplinary" approaches, led to a fruitful contextualization of law: by considering it within its economic, social, and political contexts, scholars were able to explain its evolution more fully. By inviting us to engage with the sensory and emotional turn in law, the author urges us to take a further – and indeed decisive – step: no longer a horizontal "contextualization" but a vertical "rooting," a plunge into the physical and emotional universe that lies at the source of our evaluations and normative constructions.

It is as if one were to draw a triangle whose base is formed by aesthetics and ethics, with law representing the apex. Legal theory thus appears clearly indebted to a comprehensive vision of humanity and of the society built by human beings. It is on this plane that Plato situates himself in the *Protagoras* when he recounts that the secret of the laws ensuring concord within cities rests on *aidos* and *dike*: two political affections, two inclinations toward civilization, two "transcendental conditions," in Kant's language, for the successful passage to law.

In different terms, one might say that this book calls for a "reincarnation" of law: formal and procedural law, positive and state-based, impersonal and abstract, is urged to live again and recover its colors. To the appeal of the

Other, especially when weaker or suffering, juridical conscience is summoned to respond – to become responsible (from the Latin *respondere*).

To this end, it is necessary to cultivate a form of "listening," a sensory and affective sensibility from which the constructions of modern law have often estranged us. Our codes are populated by abstract figures connected only in general terms. This formalism, characteristic of the emergence of law, has undeniable advantages – the emancipation from the possible constraints and attachments of basic social relations, the generalization, and hence, the equalization of solutions – but it also carries the risk of personal disengagement and ethical indifference.

The invitation to a "reincarnation" of law, therefore, renews the ethical demand addressed to it. It is no longer a matter merely of satisfying the (formal) "legality" of a solution, nor even its "justice," but of seeking its "rightness," understood as an attunement of the sensibilities at stake in a dispute or, more broadly, within social relations.

Here, then, is the aim: to conceive of an "embodied" law from the perspective of the "rightness" of its responses.

The pages that follow have no other ambition than to accompany the path of this reflection in the form of a cooperative dialog that, along the way, will pose certain questions and suggest a few extensions in order to make the text both resonate and reason (*résonner* and *raisonner*).

In the introduction, the framework, object, and ambition of the work are set out. The framework is that of a renewed appreciation for the sensibility of thought.

Here, the author introduces one of the book's recurring themes: the ambivalent nature of sensibility, which is at once indebted to bodily limitation and marked by openness – by the capacity for affectivity and, therefore, by a preliminary apprehension of the Other and of what lies beyond.

Understood in this way, sensibility is a threshold (a word that recurs frequently throughout the book), a springboard, a condition of access to the Other, to others, to the city, and, more broadly, to the living world. This form of sensibility is immediately tied to an ethical dimension, since the openness in question is conceived not in a sensualist, materialist, or behaviorist sense, as in many contemporary studies, but rather as an ethical capacity for affection – the ability to let oneself be "touched" by the Other.

Although this book is devoted to law, one may legitimately ask what law has to do with a sensibility that brings us to the boundaries of ourselves and makes us feel our limits. The point, as the author rightly shows, is that law is precisely the art of forming bonds while ensuring respect for limits. Law is a matter of boundaries; it is the art of measure, the discernment of right proportions. For this reason – and this is indeed the ambition of the work – it is urgent to remind jurists that their practice depends not only on technique but also on art: the art of determining the right measure, capable of offering a "responsible" (or, as some American authors put it, "responsive") response.

In the first chapter, this reflection is situated within the modern and contemporary context of Western culture, marked by the dominance of technology. The aim is by no means anti-scientific; rather, it seeks to "re-enchant" calculating reason and to restore dialog between the two poles of human reason by reintegrating into this concert the voice of sensitive reason and imagination – to reincarnate, once again, a form of reason that has too often become "hemiplegic."

From the very beginning, man has been marked by artificiality: as in the fable of Protagoras – and this is the tale's first lesson – mankind survives only thanks to Prometheus's theft of fire and the techniques that accompany it. It has often been observed that the human creature has no nature of its own but is what it becomes. Less constrained than other living beings by natural determinism, it falls to man to give sense to and transform the parameters of his condition.

In other words, culture – which also includes technology – is, for man, a second nature, a constructed nature for which he is largely responsible. Yet the naturalness of this necessity should not make us lose sight of the grounding of human culture in the sensitive and bodily condition that man shares with other living beings.

Nevertheless, since Descartes, Western reason has never ceased to sharpen the dualism between body ("extended substance") and mind ("thinking substance"), a divide that continues today and finds reinforcement in transhumanist fantasies – dreaming, through the engineering of the "augmented body," of freeing itself from death, the ultimate limit.

By radicalizing artifice, this binary mode of thinking becomes a thought "under equal conditions": it can ensure the success of its models only at the cost of a radical suspension of the external world. But the world will not be sealed beneath a glass dome; reality asserts its own rights, and it is the mark of an embodied mode of thinking to recall this – especially in the face of binary, calculating rationality, now operationalized through algorithms and computers, which produce a dominant form of reasoning and governance, making all the more urgent a bodily reinscription of our being in the world.

The aim is not to replace Descartes's radical rationalism with a form of radical sensualism – an *I feel, therefore I am* in place of *cogito ergo sum*. As the author has already emphasized, her appeal to sensibility is as much ethical as it is sensory (and within the sensory turn, this differentiation between an empiricist dimension and an ethical or esthetic one could itself be the subject of fruitful inquiry).

It is not, therefore, a matter of reasoning in terms of mere sensory stimuli, but of mobilizing the vast domain of emotions – those reactions that, quite literally, set us in motion (from the Latin *e-movere*). Recent studies have shown that, without emotions, human beings are incapable of making decisions, regardless of the extent of their knowledge – a lesson that judges would do well to consider.

At this point, it is most fitting to call on the testimony of artists and poets, for they are the ones who have never forgotten the constitutive role of that feeling which the binary world of calculation would prefer to repress entirely. By reconnecting with this vital dimension, the poet works to make language live again – "to give a purer meaning to the words of the tribe," as Mallarmé wrote (*donner un sens plus pur aux mots de la tribu*).

The poet's words prove sensitive to the condition of the Other, standing at the margins of preconception; they can echo those forms of suffering that find no expression in official registers – what Lyotard called the *différend*, which leaves the victim voiceless, unable to access the authorized codes, and of which, as he wrote, literature ought instead to be the "vigilant guardian."

For the artist – and for the responsible jurist who takes up the torch – the challenge is to give form to those voices that come from outside: to transform perceived meaning into a form that can be shared and made significant.

Reflection thus leads to a consideration of cultural forms that could be compared with Cassirer's theses (the philosophy of "symbolic forms") and with Wittgenstein's (the philosophy of "forms of life"). One might also imagine a philosophy of "style," of the different ways of "being in the world." Or, following the author, one may return to revisit the meaning of *techne*, protecting it from the domineering and predatory *hybris* to which the Greeks were so sensitive, and linking it instead to the art of the Muses, which opens what is unsayable and not yet known.

This openness also has an ethical dimension.

The Other, toward whom this sensibility opens, is not an alter ego – that would be merely another self; we would remain enclosed within the galaxy of the one and the same, within the register of the *auto* and the *tauto* – but a true other (not totally other, for otherwise we would have nothing in common, but other enough to alter me, to make me at least in part other: "oneself as another," in Ricoeur's powerful expression).

In short, it is a matter of participating in a being-in-the-world that does justice both to the singularity of persons and to their shared belonging – to the realm of the living, to the city, to our common humanity.

The author once again proposes this beautiful formula: *ego cum* rather than *ego sum* – a condition in which the human being is exposed to the risk of the Other, in the awareness that to withdraw from this affection (the word is significant, for it evokes affectivity) is to fall into meaninglessness and barbarism.

In the second chapter, the discussion turns to law in order to highlight the ways in which it may be put to "good use." This is a form of law that, in the best of cases – or according to its highest purpose – takes account of both the sensitive condition and the ethical demand already described, constructing the symbolic figure of the third: an unavailable third that nonetheless arises from the parties themselves; a third who personifies the idea of the "common" (the common good, the general interest, which is more than the individual good).

Such a conception of law should, in my view, be capable of ensuring what Ricoeur called the "long function of justice": the capacity to grant to each of the parties involved – both the victim and the presumed perpetrator – the "merited recognition" that goes beyond the simple "short function," which confines justice to restoring only what is due to each. For while the long function reestablishes social peace by inviting everyone to "take part once again" in social life, the short one contents itself with giving "to each his due," thereby restoring a mere *status quo ante* that may itself be oppressive or unjust.

This "long function" also certainly mobilizes a sensitive understanding of the situation of the parties involved. In this respect, the paradigmatic example is provided by the famous judgment of Solomon, in which the king of Israel brings the just solution to light not through the formal application of the law (which, in this case, offers no determinate solution), but through the entrails of the child's mother – who consents to an injustice so that life may prevail: "No, do not kill him; give the child to the other woman!"

As a lucid observer of the contemporary world, the author does not conceal how difficult it is for the law to attain this ideal.

The phenomenon of law shopping, for instance – where economic actors choose the legal system that best serves their particular interests – constitutes a repudiation of the very logic of the third, since in such cases the third instance of the law becomes, in a sense, privatized and instrumentalized within the balance of power that shapes basic social relations. The author conceals none of the distortions that arise, on the one hand, from the formal bureaucratization of law, nor those, on the other, that denature it when it submits to the laws of the market.

The reference to human rights likewise calls for renewed lucidity. When conceived in absolutist terms – as attributes of the sovereign subject, summed up in the maxim "the self by law, the law for me" – do they not reinforce the solipsistic logic (*solus ipse*) of an exacerbated neoliberalism? It is, therefore, urgent to reconnect rights with the idea of human dignity – the very source of both rights and responsibilities – so as to restore their effectiveness, now threatened by the dominance of economic rules.

Finally, the use of large databases and computer-assisted decision-making systems should not proceed without critical scrutiny. Although it would be absurd to dispense with them entirely, we must nevertheless not allow such technologies – substituting for the "balanced" judgment of a judge who has long hesitated before deciding – to produce a standardizing effect in judicial decisions, at the expense of juridical creativity and careful attention to the uniqueness of each case.

How can a judge resist the overwhelming number of precedents presented by the attorney of one of the parties, even when his or her own sense of justice suggests an alternative solution? Conformism and standardization are, as we know, the automatic products of the algorithms that govern search engines such as Google, which invariably direct users to the most frequently consulted sites.

To resist such drifts and to remain on the path of a "good use of law," the author draws on the advances of the broad Law and Humanities movement (useful bibliographical references, particularly on the topic of sensations and emotions, are provided in notes 3–5 to Chapter 2; see below, 36–37).

The field of emotions is currently very active, and it is therefore necessary to distinguish between "empathy" and "sympathy," between primary and secondary emotions, private and collective, real and fictitious ones. It should also be recalled that emotions are, to a large extent, products of cultural construction and are thus subject both to social determinants and to change over time. And if we agree with Sophocles, who reminds us in the first stasimon of *Antigone* that "it is passions that govern cities," we must also acknowledge that passions and emotions need to be guided, lest they destroy the social bond when driven by vengeful anger or violence.

If, for example, controlled and measured indignation can give rise to monuments such as Zola's *J'accuse*, we know all too well, by contrast, that waves of hatred on social networks provoke dangerous storytelling and forms of media lynching. (As it happens, while I was writing these pages, a friend of mine – a magistrate – sent me these few lines by Marguerite Yourcenar (1981, 294), which I cannot refrain from quoting here: "Gradually, as in all trials which temporarily excite the mob, two strangely dissimilar cases seemed to be evolving on two different levels: the cause as it appeared to men of law and to churchmen, both of whom commonly sit as judges, and the cause as fabricated by the rabble, who thirst for monsters or victims."

How, then, can we distinguish the great emancipatory narratives from the alienating and divisive scenarios of contemporary storytelling? How, if not by mobilizing some of the great figures and foundational narratives of Western culture? As happens, for example, with the figure of Temperance – whom we remember seated beside Justice in Ambrogio Lorenzetti's celebrated fresco *The Allegory of Good and Bad Government* in the Palazzo Pubblico of Siena – who moderates and reconciles conflicting sensations, emotions, interests, and values.

That Temperance inscribes itself in the long time of attention – the mediation of justice in the rule of law, as opposed to the immediacy of media justice or that of social networks – and is the indispensable companion of Prudence, the cardinal virtue of responsible jurists (its etymology is recalled: from the Latin *pro-videre*, "to see from afar"). The author traces this back to Hesiod's tale of the Horae – Eunomia, Dike, and Eirene – who preside over the just order, both the natural order of things and the constructed order of cities. These Horae evoke rhythm and measure, or again, that rightness sung by the poet and inspiring the justice of the judge.

Another foundational resource of just law is the already-evoked myth of Prometheus and Epimetheus. Plato reminds us that mastery of technique alone is not enough to guarantee the survival of cities; on the contrary, human beings never cease to fight among themselves because they do not share the *philia* that "serves as a rule for the cities." For this reason, a concerned Zeus ultimately sends his faithful messenger Hermes to mankind – not to impose a ready-made code of laws but, more importantly, to offer them the very conditions of sociality: *dike* and *aidos*.

Dike is that sense of justice which the author understands, above all, as the will and capacity to create and sustain bonds (as opposed to *adikia*, the self-enclosed withdrawal that breeds discord – the false note that ruins the sought-after harmony). And *aidos*, a complex and subtle notion (closest perhaps to "respect"), has its roots in the most intimate dimension of sensibility, presupposing something like modesty or restraint – a relation both open and attentive, a necessary condition for human interactions that honor the expectations of the other. Understood as the capacity to engage in relationships that forge bonds while respecting limits, *aidos*, as will now be clear, is the (pre-)juridical affection *par excellence*.

The story is exemplary in more than one sense. It also shows that, while among animals the distribution of qualities (by Epimetheus) is natural and unequal, among human beings the distribution of social affections (*aidos* and *dike*) is, by contrast, cultural and egalitarian. All have received them in the obligatory sharing that binds society together, such that whoever departs from them becomes subject to sanction. Hence the idea – responding to the initial question that gives rise to the myth – that political and juridical art is not so much the object of *a priori* instruction as of a *paideia* practiced daily through lived experience.

This reference, finally, leads back to the daily practice of a "sensitive law," nourished and inspired by the work of art, defined by the author as every work-made-with-art, whatever its expressive form and whatever artistic or cultural genre it may belong to – understanding by this any work capable of initiating a process of opening to sense, that is, of opening the transformative space of experience.

The aim of the third chapter is precisely to present several encounters with works of art in order to illustrate how the refinement of esthetic and ethical sensibility can help shape the juridical measure closest to rightness.

Eight such encounters, the fruit of the author's teaching practice, form something like a toolbox – or rather a treasure chest – of evocations: paintings, films, philosophical meditations, and juridical reflections, all intended to set in motion (*e-movere*) the creative imagination of the responsible jurist. For it is the task of the responsible jurist to put himself into action, avoiding the temptation to practice law casually, as though it were merely a formal technique to which one could remain a stranger.

An active agent within the "limit" of social bonds, the capable jurist intervenes as an "interpreter" of discourses blocked by conflict, as an interface between "subsystems" (Walzer speaks of "spheres of justice"; Boltanski and Thévenot of "cities") that always risk remaining enclosed within their own logic. Such should be, for example, the lawyer as a "representative" of his client – one who shares the client's cause with sensibility while maintaining the necessary distance to allow the emergence of the third voice (that of the judge, of the law) needed to untie the knot of conflict.

Each of the encounters proposed represents, in its own way, an experience of limits – limits that, like boundaries or skin, as the author has shown, are at once a barrier (inevitable and protective) and a site of exchange and openness to the outside. And if it is true that law is the art of negotiating limits, we can clearly perceive what is at stake in these experiences.

Without claiming to be exhaustive, I recall here the boundary between the human and the sacred in Beato Angelico's *Annunciation*; the confrontation with the animal and the robot in Sapochnik's film *Finch*; the experience of mechanical brutality in Kafka's *In the Penal Colony*; the tragic condition of the *entre-deux* and the *no man's land* of migrants, suspended between two worlds and a land of no one; the limits of nonsense explored through confinement within social conventions in Musil's *The Man Without Qualities*; and finally, the rich boundaries of silence and of the unsayable in the meditations of Jabès (one might think here of blindfolded Justice: what does she see through her inner gaze?).

It is impossible, in this space, to do justice to the richness of these various evocations. I will confine myself to commenting briefly on two of them.

Beato Angelico's *Annunciation*, brought into resonance with a poem by Rilke, illustrates particularly well the book's approach, which, as I have said, attempts a kind of incarnation of law – the juridical word is called upon to become flesh in order to keep its promises. The author's fine analysis of the fresco, which opens onto the infinite and the sacred through and from the limits of the cell (of the Virgin and of the convent of San Marco), could usefully be compared with the beautiful analyses that Merleau-Ponty devoted precisely to the "flesh of the world," with his way of presenting our being-in-the-world, and in particular our condition as sentient beings engaged in what he called the "chiasm of the visible" (the one who sees and the one who is seen ceaselessly exchanging positions).

My second observation concerns Kafka's *In the Penal Colony*. The story is, of course, horrifying, and it can be read as a depiction of a possible refinement of cruelty. Yet I cannot help reading between the lines an evocation – difficult, even paradoxical – of the idea that the suffering body is also a condition of access to knowledge and, as such, a step toward liberation. This is attested by the condemned man's expectant elation: he learns the sentence only once it has been completely inscribed on his body, and in that final hour, he is reunited with the community and its law. This suggests, therefore, that the true horror of the tale, as reported by the traveler, lies rather in the fact that, once the machine has been dismantled forever, the individual is henceforth destined to remain radically cut off from that knowledge and from his community.

Kafka's *Diaries* overflow with references to this learning through the suffering body, suggesting yet another aspect – again difficult and paradoxical, I admit – of a bodily conception of law.

It is clear that Paola Mittica's book is one that invites reading and rereading. One must patiently meditate on its silences, allowing its spoken and unspoken words to resonate for a long time. My hope is that, after finding its readers, it will become the object of further discussion and expansion – of which only a few possible directions have been evoked here. The challenge it poses is essential: to articulate the link between the law taught in universities (too often formalist) or practiced in the field (too often reduced to pragmatic urgencies or economic interests) and the sensitive law evoked in this book, in search of the most fitting measure of justice.

François Ost
Jurist and Philosopher, Professor Emeritus at UCLouvain–Saint-Louis (Brussels), and Member of the Royal Academy of Belgium

Translator's Note

Unless otherwise stated, all translations in this volume are my own. Where authoritative English translations were available, these have been consulted and adopted, and are referenced in the bibliography. In all other cases, the translations are mine.

Introduction

Feeling is what moves us. All understanding is permeated by feeling – by the restlessness that animates it. Sensibility is another way of naming thought – or rather, of naming thinking itself – in order to restore it to its condition as body, and thus as limit. For the prudent jurist, devoted to discerning the right measure, every limit is a threshold.

The thinking of the body consists in preparing oneself for the coming of sense. It is tension – an openness without object, an act of listening, of attentiveness, of awaiting. A finite thought, yet open in its striving toward the infinite – one that arises from the sensitive encounter with the Other, with the Thou, with something or someone.

The search for sense that opens within the space of alterity is perhaps the most authentically juridical of all, for it is in law that we locate thirdness as the guardian of what surpasses the original relation between I and Thou: the common, the axis upon which we build our world. A being-in-common that is third, since it concerns the reasons of relation – rather than those of individuals – from the perspective of a project of human and solidaristic coexistence; and, at the same time, the reasons for the commitment to care for other living beings and, more generally, for the natural environment, seeking to temper the excesses of the unsustainable world of the human species.

Law is the object of this inquiry: a transformative movement, a sensitive experience – at once feeling, sentiment, and reasoning – that becomes sense as it takes shape in forms that render the limit visible and recognizable, forms intended to contain the expansion of human individuality. Yet, it is a function that risks being irretrievably lost with the completion of the bureaucratization of the world, among whose distortions one of the most evident is the reduction of law to a dehumanized mechanism.

The reflection guiding these pages asks, in essence, how to live the limit through art in order to listen to – and to speak – the law.

The work is structured into three chapters.

The first begins by examining the original relationship that the human being weaves with culture and technique, opening up the gap between technical rationality and other forms of human intelligence. Its aim is to recover the full range of the human creature's cognitive resources and to integrate them into an idea of sensibility embodied in the thinking of the body.

This form of intelligence corresponds to a more complex technical capacity – one that, following Aristotle's distinction, brings together both "technical creativity," which involves scientific and technological knowledge in the strict sense, and "creative technique," that is, poetic *techne*.

Such an art could preside over the creation of forms as thresholds – forms capable of making possible the coming of sense, understood fundamentally as the feeling of the Other. In these terms, the esthetic perspective could be introduced as sensitive knowledge and, by reflecting on forms as thresholds upon alterity, be brought into dialog with ethics.

The second chapter, employing the same conceptual framework, identifies the elements necessary to construct a reflection that accounts for the close relationship between sensibility and law, engaging with the ongoing debate on Law and Aesthetics and the use of the Law and Humanities methodology, particularly in support of legal education.

On this subject, while referring to current studies, the aim is to offer a contribution by examining three notions that emerge from the history of Western culture like fossils, revealing the original kinship between law and poetic art, between aesthetics and ethics – that is, between sensitive knowledge, the orientation toward the good, and the capacity to look to the future. This section concludes with a discussion of the art of law – that is, of the capable jurist.

The third and final chapter turns to a number of Law and Humanities experiments that I have had the opportunity to conduct and share in my regular university teaching, through courses and workshops with law students.

The aim is to present, as clearly and vividly as possible, the kinds of practices implied in the idea of integrating legal education. And since an encounter with a complex form requires preparation, these experiences are preceded by a few reflections on what it means to engage with a work of art.

Before concluding, I wish to say that this work is the result of many encounters – with colleagues who, over the years, have become valued traveling companions, and with the intellectual stimuli from which I have greatly benefited and to which I am indebted – not least to María José Falcón y Tella, whose determination made this translation possible, and to Mark Byrne, who carried it out.

I am especially grateful to François Ost for engaging in dialog with me on these themes and for contributing more than one insight for further reflection; and to Daniele Cananzi for welcoming this work – born in Italian – into the series of the *Centro di ricerca di Estetica del diritto* (CRED), and for continuing to support it in this new version, which includes, as an appendix, a previously unpublished essay on Cormac McCarthy's last two novels. To Angelo, to whom the book is dedicated, I owe the gift of his steadfast presence.

The responsibility for this work is mine alone. The pages that follow bear witness to the many thresholds I have inhabited, aware that I was touching on different fields, each marked by a high degree of specialization. Rather than fearing disciplinary transgressions, I chose to follow the impulse to dwell also in a necessary elsewhere, so as not to renounce the possibility of departing from the forms of knowledge most familiar to me and of attempting a method of research. From precariousness, from uncertainty, from naïve discoveries, I believe I have learned to feel more deeply.

CHAPTER 1

Naturally Artificial

1 Ecology of the Future

Any reflection on law that claims to have value must first inquire into certain essential questions concerning human life – above all, the idea of man as a living being and the context in which he comes into existence and fulfills himself.

In a detailed reconstruction of Western anthropology, Arnold Gehlen offers a penetrating analysis of the original relationship between man, culture, and technique.

Because of a series of biological deficiencies, according to Gehlen (1988), man comes into the world originally lacking the specializations necessary for survival in any natural environment. He is inferior to other animal species in the sharpness of his senses and instincts; he has no claws for hunting or defense, no gills for breathing underwater, no body adapted to cold or heat, and lacks the various attributes that characterize other living beings populating the Earth.

In other words, he is born into a place that is not made for him, just as he is not made for it. He finds himself there as if in a storm – submerged by myriads of stimuli, prey to unconscious impulses, in a state of total bewilderment.

And yet, it is precisely this deficiency – which exposes man to the risk of not surviving – that places him in a condition of openness to the world, enabling him to find the path toward emancipation from his biological limitation while, at the same time, exercising an ever-expanding dominion over the natural environment.

Referring to Gehlen's thought, Galimberti (1999, 160 ff.) explains that, unlike other animals – endowed with specialized instincts that respond to stimuli determined by rigidly fixed environmental conditions – man, precisely because he is incomplete in both anatomical–functional structure and instinctual specialization, has the advantage of not being bound by constraints that predefine his behavior.

Thus, once he comes into life, that same world which torments him with its indecipherability paradoxically also presents itself as a field of endless surprises that may hold countless positive possibilities. The generality of his instincts, rather than a weakness, in fact, proves to be his greatest resource, for it translates into a polyvalent capacity for adaptation – *plasticity*, in Geh-

 | HTTPS://DOI.ORG/10.1163/9789004757714-003

len's terminology – that enables him to develop the techniques necessary for existence anywhere, discovering within nature itself the means of survival.

In this way, the human creature selects the possibilities most favorable to its own existence and stabilizes them into suitable living environments.

> Openness to the world and plasticity in adaptation make the human being a creature that "accomplishes itself," that "does not merely live but leads its life," in the sense that its life depends on the "construction" it makes of it. In this sense, Gehlen defines the human being as "a creature that takes a position," through procedures of *selection and stabilization* by which it achieves "culturally" that selectivity and stability which the animal, by instinct, possesses by nature.
>
> In that "field of infinite surprises" that is the world, human beings, through their successes and failures, either overlook or adopt, from the profusion of stimuli to which they are open, those responses advantageous to life which – once connected and stabilized – form the fabric of memory that then becomes the basis of projection. (Galimberti 1999, 163)

The adaptation in question is cultural, since it derives from man's capacity to distance himself from the pressure of environmental stimuli and from his own impulses. Thanks to this distancing, which releases him from the burden of the profusion of stimuli to which he is open, man succeeds in grasping a comprehensive – *panoramic*, in Gehlen's terms – vision of the world, necessary for elaborating the fields of possibility within which to orient his life projects. In this process, there is no separation between the external and the internal world: adaptation to the natural environment also functions as a disciplining of impulses, running through all cognitive processes, from perception to the most evolved forms of language.

All the vitality of man is directed toward creating the conditions for his own life, and he does so out of natural necessity – through culture, that is, through the creation of artifices that Gehlen calls *allusions*.

> The entire vital purpose [...] consists, in fact, in "disjoining" "actions" from "drives" and "needs" [...] through the containment and reduction of instincts, or rather "through the inversion of the direction of the drives." (Cometa 2020, 237)

Man is not, therefore, a creature endowed in the abstract with spirit. He is a being lacking specific instincts, who reacts to his inadequacy through an innate technical capacity that enables him to equip himself, constructing both himself and his world.

In this sense, there is no separation between technique, culture, and nature. Spirit is not independent of the body or of the natural world. Culture is, for man, a second skin:

> The epitome of nature restructured to serve his needs is called *culture*, and the cultural world is the human world. [...] The cultural world exists for man in exactly the same way in which the environment exists for an animal. For this reason alone, it is wrong to speak of an environment, in a strictly biological sense, for man. His world-openness is directly related to his unspecialized structure; similarly, his lack of physical means corresponds directly to his self-created "second nature." (Gehlen 1988, 27–30)

The technical capacity to which Gehlen refers is entirely oriented toward action. It manifests as activity directed toward building and producing. Its principal resource is rational intelligence – the only faculty capable of reversing the direction of the drives, containing passions, reducing stimuli, and thereby disentangling complex sentiments; in other words, identifying one's own chances for life.

Technique and rationality permeate the environment of possibilities available to man: a world diminished in relation to the true world – vast and polymorphous – which becomes sustainable only when circumscribed by rational action within precise boundaries that delimit, above all, knowledge.

For Gehlen, in fact, the only knowledge possible is that which arises from action informed by technique and rationality, both dependent on biological necessity. Man can, therefore, conceive only the world he himself has constructed – the only world to which he has access and within which he can orient himself. It is for this reason that, surpassing every other cognitive resource, rationality and technique become the load-bearing axis of science.

The same mechanics govern the production of the future. Not only do technique and rationality work to transform the natural environment, adapting it to human needs; in doing so, they constantly exceed the measure dictated by the necessities of the present in order to secure a future. And this is not a matter of choice. As Gehlen puts it, "Man, whom 'even future hunger makes hungry' has 'no time' – unless he prepares for tomorrow, he will not be able to survive" (1988, 43). That is to say, he must systematically construct a portion of the world that exceeds his immediate action, allowing life to project itself beyond the present – without, however, ever stepping outside the horizon of that artificial world, the only one in which it is possible to live (Natoli 2002, 63).

This is the future of Western man as Gehlen foresees it: a mechanism animated by technique and rationality, imposing upon nature a destiny of progressive manipulation with no possibility of return – a destiny marked by excess.

Undoubtedly, this is a fascinating thesis that, regardless of the radicality with which it is formulated, helps us to understand both the reasons that have guided man's predominance over nature and the growing rationalization that characterizes the development of what we call civilization – without, however, proving deceptive in its predicted outcomes. This is especially true if it is used to reread the history of Western man in modernity, in both its rise and its decline, and to grasp the paradoxical results of our current model of life and society.

To the fundamental theories of classical sociology – especially those of the Weberian tradition – Gehlen's anthropology adds, in other words, further grounds for observing the crisis that has overtaken the contemporary world, making still more evident the fact that the environments we have built to live in are the perfect reflection of a technostructure that strengthens itself in step with the bureaucratization of the world – a process whose meshes encompass every aspect of life through the close interrelation between society, the political system, the capitalist economy, and science (Ventura 2020).[1]

The paradox is that, in this process, the technostructure – while conveying an ever-growing number of rational selections governed by a technique further enhanced by technology – simultaneously multiplies the possibilities of choices that endanger the very well-being the system claims to promote, to the point of threatening the survival of the human species itself. Nor, to use Luhmann's categories, does it seem possible to maintain that technology effectively meets the imperative of reducing increasing complexity. Indeed, in a society of low complexity, technology develops without major problems or dilemmas, whereas in a society of high complexity, every solution almost always reformulates itself as a new problem (Natoli 2002).

---

1 Denouncing the structural flaws of the Enlightenment – the Promethean project of rationalizing the world – Ventura emphasizes how bureaucratization affects every aspect of life: economic, political, social, cultural, artistic, and symbolic. In this sense, he draws on Debord's well-known view – according to which contemporary Western society essentially coincides with the bureaucratization of production and consumption: a spectacle of an economy that administers things and people, a dominant science and a science of domination – to highlight an even more serious fact, namely that the Western model is regarded as the best form of society on a global scale, leaving no possibility of escaping the horizon of a single ideology: the identical cult of progress and the sole motive of capital accumulation (Ventura 2020, 77–79).

Moreover, technology based on artificial intelligence generates more possibilities than man can manage; the same applies to the purchasing possibilities of commodities within the capitalist economy – and even within the markets of culture, science, and politics.

In short, as the bureaucratization of life advances, systematically exceeding all measure, the world becomes increasingly complex and difficult to order. On the other hand, if the attention of the human being has been entirely drawn within the boundaries of the technostructure and its forms of knowledge, it is easy to understand how life has been suffocated by the anxiety of survival.[2]

Natoli is right to redefine our contemporaneity not so much as the age of technology but as the age of risk – where the danger lies, above all, in the fact that, by placing itself at the center of the world stage, technology has overtaken every other cognitive potential of the human creature, with the result that man finds himself in a condition of risk that he neither recognizes nor knows how to confront:

> Technology is therefore dangerous not so much because of what it brings into operation – let us say, because of its consequences – but because it conceals human beings from themselves, keeping them enclosed within the horizon of domination as their only horizon of possibility. (Natoli 2002, 66)

Not only, as Gehlen clearly explains, does the domination of technology prevent a disenchanted view of the world – because it itself determines what man can see – but, by feeding faith in the capacity to think scientifically and to invent new technologies, it progressively weakens other fundamental resources for understanding, such as perceptual and affective faculties, thereby producing a form of estrangement of man from himself (Bollas 2018).

A further, and perhaps more insidious, effect of this mechanism is that it subtly acts upon the affective and instinctual sphere of man, exploiting vulnerabilities, channeling fears and unconscious desires, and feeding to excess the will to power realized through social affirmation or, more trivially, through the consumption of any commodity – material or symbolic – at every level.

This profoundly shapes human reflection on man and on the meaning of his being-in-the-world. Every aspect of our existence is conceivable and share-

2 Relevant in this regard are Han's reflections on the absolutization of survival orchestrated by the neoliberal system, brought further to light by the recent pandemic crisis (Han 2021, 22).

able only within a representation – within the finite horizon of symbolic mediation.

We think, evaluate, plan, desire, and suffer; we nourish illusions and ambitions, endure disappointments, and become angry when we do not receive due recognition. The feelings and passions that agitate us – our thoughts, everything – are the product of this artifice.

The clearest proof of this lies in the manipulation of pain. Bureaucratization works pervasively and preemptively to optimize life and remove pain, masking the appearance of well-being as the good life. It deceives pain, displacing it from the positive horizon of existence. It disguises it because the limit embodied by pain would contradict the will to power that the reason of the technostructure must instead cultivate in man in order to advance its project of domination.

Deprived of the capacity to recognize consciously a discontinuity within a mechanism that has overtaken him, man – no longer aware of limit – cannot perceive risk, nor can he resist the excess to which technology exposes him. With no resources other than calculating reason, unable to glimpse anything beyond this machinery, the human creature cannot imagine a future other than that of the life of the technostructure.

In Jonas's effective description (1984), *homo faber*, having become the object of technology, turns his art upon himself, ingeniously preparing to redesign even the artificer, until he has finally surpassed himself.

The vision is dramatic and intentionally provocative. For Jonas, the challenge that ethical thought must confront is to turn back from the irresponsibility that the mechanics of bureaucracy have erected into a system – to reclaim for itself the task of living, and of living as human beings. It is a duty toward existence: an authentic humanity that must be recovered in order to be transmitted to future generations, as Elena Pulcini (2009) insightfully observes.

The age of technology (Galimberti 1999). The age of risk (Natoli 2002). The age of bewilderment (Bollas 2018). All tell of the failure of the Enlightenment project of the emancipation of Western man – and of the ruin that advances rapidly.

Yet it is not over, and the proof lies in the widespread dissatisfaction that many of us feel – though muted or disguised by the innumerable *pharmaka* that the technostructure makes available to us.

In the age of well-being at any cost, unease also grows – and it is precisely this malaise that most opens reflection on a different possible future. Its signs can be read in the anxiety or melancholy impressed upon the gazes that surface through the masks sculpted and imposed by conventional culture, without our being able to grasp a precise or defined cause; but also in the work of those who take charge of that unease, using it as a crowbar to gain critical distance from dominant meanings.

With persistence, a new awareness thus emerges, finding space among folds, cracks, fractures, and interstices of consolidated meaning, and once again questioning human beings about life on this side of its concealment.

For Jullien (2020), *true life* resists obscuration by the constraining apparatus of civilization, by social conformism, or by the opinions and options that constantly clutter it. The question, then, is how one might approach it, how one might come close to it again, and where it might be rediscovered.

There are many pages to leaf through, marked by restlessness, scattered throughout our languages – and especially within artistic ones, as we shall see. But a word of caution.

To debunk the myth of technology as a project of salvation, to expose its paradoxical face and its fallacy, and to reveal its potential for risk does not mean denying the technical capacity innate to man, nor nostalgically yearning for a naïve return to nature. Man is a naturally artificial animal, and we must remain "aware that an ecology can only be a technology" (Nancy 1997a).

What matters, rather, is to recover a proper measure of ourselves and of our existence, in order to begin once again to reflect – hopefully with more fitting keys – on our world: to build it, to inhabit it, and to hand it on to those who will come after us.

On the one hand, it is a matter of reviving thought (Bollas 2018), distancing ourselves from the absolutism of technical rationality, which has become so powerful that it risks no longer being governed by human intelligence. On the other hand, since there is no way out of the horizon of technology, reflection must once again turn to technology as an original and inescapable resource for man – to understand not only whether and to what extent it can be rebalanced, but also, and above all, to consider other modes of technique that might be drawn upon, and to bring their potential to light (or perhaps, better said, into *chiaroscuro*).

On the first front, what is at stake is the possibility of opening up a distance (*écarter*) between technical rationality and other forms of human intelligence, and thus between technostructure and body. On the second front, reflection must turn to art.

2 The Thinking of the Body

The vision of man as a naturally artificial being not only culminates in the complete overcoming of the dualism between nature and culture but also powerfully shifts the point of view, placing the body at the center of reflection – of man, on man, and for man.[3] It thus leads us to the question that most concerns us: fundamentally, whether it is possible to think by drawing upon the body – or, better, whether it is possible to rethink thought itself by recognizing, in the body's sensibility, genuine cognitive resources on which to rely for understanding our existence and our making of the world.

In other words, can the foreshortening produced by technical rationality be overcome by a more complex apprehension of the world – one that man might experience through an intelligence that is also sensitive, integrating the many forms of human intelligence?

The idea of man reduced to a system of observation – perhaps the most radical evolution of rationalism, which Luhmann also derives from Gehlen's theoretical framework – is not, in fact, sufficient to dispel the doubt that the global crisis engulfing our world may also stem from the loss of significant portions of human intelligence, to the point that we can no longer draw fully upon our cognitive resources, if not entirely, then at least in part, to distance ourselves from the systems of the technostructure and its bureaucracy.

Ultimately, we must ask whether the experience that man has of the world and of himself as body leads to a broader experience – that is, to a kind of understanding capable of opening beyond meaning reduced to the artificial mediation within which the horizon of predetermined possibilities is exhausted.

If we do not wish to contract human experience, revising the reductive definition of man as *animal rational* is, after all, an operation that can no longer be postponed – particularly when we speak of law (Campanale 2016, 75).

To the question, "What idea of man?" posed in the opening pages of his *Philosophy of the Will*, Ricoeur (1966, 9–10) replies that the reconquest of the *Cogito* must be total, specifying that within the meaning of the *Cogito* we must rediscover the body and the involuntary that it sustains.

If the idea of man is anchored to that of the sentient being, then what changes is the very meaning of "sentient." In other words, the capacity for knowledge that must be recovered is that which can comprehend every quality of our *intelligere*, becoming once again body itself, down to the involuntary – that which the body nourishes and which does not always emerge into consciousness, which lives beneath the surface and likely moves us, conditioning our judgments and the actions that follow, even when these appear "rational."

3 In this sense, Gehlen's thesis aligns with the critique of the numerous categorical oppositions that stem from the fracture between *logos* and *bios* and that mark the history of Western philosophical, political, and legal thought (Esposito 2015).

There should be no search for the primacy of the ontological over the cognitive, nor, conversely, of the cognitive over the ontological: "the integral experience of the *Cogito* embraces the I desire, the I can, the I live, and, in general, existence as body" (*ibid.*).

"The body *makes room* for existence [...] [It] *is* the being of existence," Nancy summarizes (2008a, 15). Recovering the unity of the *Cogito* as body even in Descartes himself (Nancy 2004), he calls for the urgent re-grounding of thought in all its physicality: a heavy thought, capable of restoring to meaning the density and opacity necessary for understanding (Nancy 2008b).

The body, then, thinks. But what kind of thought is it?

To begin with, thought does not coincide with rationality. The latter is only one of the possible forms of intelligence, which itself should not be defined solely according to the criteria of positive science (Jonas 1984).

> The mistake we have made so far has been to believe that the brain is the seat of a particular intelligence – indeed, of the only possible intelligence: rational intelligence. Yet rational intelligence, as such, in its pure state, is an invention of our culture. True thought is always physical, emotional. Disembodied thought does not exist in nature. (Manacorda 2016, 30)

Thought cannot be abstracted from the physicality of the body. It is sensibility. For that very reason, thought feels – and it feels within the body in its entirety.

This, of course, is nothing new. The sentient quality of the body – and thus sensible knowledge and the sensorial root of thought – is a theme that has always occupied an important place in the history of Western philosophy and culture (Borutti 2006). Even in the mid-eighteenth century, while modernity condemned feeling as a danger to the great project of emancipating humanity from its natural limits – entrusted to Enlightenment rationality – there arose the discordant voice of Cabanis, who set the notion of *sensibilité* against the Cartesian *Cogito* of his contemporaries. As Moravia (1995, 19) recalls, for Cabanis awareness of being in the world, of existence itself, derives not from thought but, more originally, from sensibility: "C'est du moment que nous sentons que nous sommes," the celebrated motto of the French physician and philosopher.

Encompassing every dimension of feeling, sensibility is anchored by Cabanis in the "living materiality of the *organisation physique*," that is, in corporeality, where the living – understood as sensibility itself – appears as "the primary energy, the founding force of life."

The human being is thus, first and foremost, an organism whose prime mover is sensibility – understood, following Cabanis, as feeling in all its tonalities (affective, perceptive, and even rational). Sensibility underlies everything that is vital for human existence, from the most immediate and instinctual expressions of corporeality to those that are culturally mediated, which must nonetheless be understood as expressions of embodied life.

To answer our question, then, we may begin by saying that the thought of the body arises from bodily experience itself, as sensibility engaging every dimension of feeling.

The word that defines this experience is “synesthesia.”

From the Greek *syn*, “together,” and *aisthánesthai*, “to perceive,” synesthesia may first be understood as the reciprocal interference among sensations belonging to different sensory spheres (Natoli 2010a, 151).

Within a vast and complex field of research that encompasses much of the human sciences – from physiology to neuroscience and psychology, from philosophy to the semiotics of perception, from literature to the arts – synesthesia has had a varied history throughout a long tradition of studies.

Sometimes regarded as a pathology, at other times as a normal function of the brain, and yet at others as an enhancement of the possibilities of connection among various formal languages, it is a phenomenon that has had the undeniable merit of bringing, once again, to the forefront – particularly in the epistemological debate of the second half of the twentieth century – the theme of sensation, and therefore of the body, raising the question of the relationship between feeling and thought, and between sense and language (De Blasio 2011).

In the sense that concerns us here, synesthesia appears as a complex, multicomponent process expressing the real simultaneity with which we experience the world through the senses, involving both the sphere of perception and that of affectivity, to which we refer our emotions. More specifically, synesthesia bears witness to the human capacity to generate sense by drawing on the full complexity of feeling. The proof lies in the trace it leaves within language itself.

Manacorda writes that synesthesia:

> is like a Jurassic shell that has remained embedded in language. A shell whose sound, over the last two centuries, has been heard only by poets. Synesthesia is the linguistic concretion of the fall (or should I say the nonexistence) of boundaries between sight, hearing, touch, smell, knowledge, and thought. (Manacorda 2016, 34)

What is affirmed here invites at least three reflections.

Described through the metaphor of a fossil shell preserved in language, synesthesia is a sensory experience that is, first and foremost, related to expressive forms – something that has never ceased to exist or to reemerge through language – allowing us to intuit that feeling, which becomes sense through its capacity to be articulated in some form of language, is present in every form.

The second reflection concerns the shell itself, whose sound, over the last two centuries, has been heard only by poets. In other words, in an era when the technostructure has reached the height of its trajectory, the feeling of the body has remained unheard by all except poets, who alone, according to Manacorda, are capable of grasping, in and through language, a sense that proceeds from a more complex form of feeling.

Finally, the notion of synesthesia proposed here clarifies that this process involves the entirety of feeling, which also encompasses knowledge and thought.

In summary, if synesthesia is the linguistic concretion of the collapse – or even the absence – of boundaries between sight, hearing, touch, smell, knowledge, and thought, then it may be said that every movement of feeling – sensory perception, emotion, thought, understanding – participates in the sense that coagulates and takes form through language.

And so, returning to our question: what kind of thought is the thought of the body that thinks?

Emerging from sensibility, we might describe it as the capacity to listen to feeling – an attentiveness awakened by the ensemble of sensations and emotions through which we experience the world, a tension to perceive and to recognize the body's feeling within the sense that gradually takes form through language.

It is, therefore, less a thought than a thinking that moves along the traces of feeling left in the forms of the world – a thinking that attends (that is, tends toward) a sense more complex than that reduced to the conventional meanings conveyed by those forms: a sense that feels, that takes shape through synesthesia, and that is not exhausted within the closed forms of languages structured by the bureaucracy of the technostructure.

By freeing itself, at least in part, from finite sense, this thinking remains mobile – open with respect to convention, and thus capable of subverting established codes, or at least deviating from them – making possible, in relation to dominant representations, a precious discontinuity in which to stretch itself in order to glimpse a different sense and a different future.

Such thinking, which does not bind itself to finite sense but rather introduces a distance from it in order to dispose itself toward the coming of sense, is the kind of thinking capable of conceiving finitude. Nancy (2003) affirms this repeatedly, indicating corporeality as an essential quality of thought.

From this perspective, the thought of the body is a thinking of the body, within the body, and from the body.

It follows that sense, too, can only be the outcome of sensitive experience. We are bodies immersed in an environment. We are exposed – bodies that are touched and that touch other bodies. Aroused by feeling, thinking is a movement that occurs in contact – with something or someone – in touching and in being touched.

From touch, then, arises sense as it emerges from the experience of the Other, of that which lies beyond the self. The Other is the living being in general, but also the Thou. For Nancy, sense exists only in relation to an "outside" or an "elsewhere," and consists precisely in this relation to what exceeds the self (Nancy 1997a).

The Other, or the Thou, which reflects – like a mirror – our finitude, makes us aware of the limits of our being and existence. But that is not all.

The touch of the Other opens a necessary space in which a form of thinking capable of feeling can unfold. This is a vital *between* for a thought that can move beyond the "already given" only insofar as it relates to another – an outside, within the enduring alterity of each being and each thing (Jullien 2018a). In the distance of what remains to be thought, "thought is the experience of this gravity and this withdrawal" (Nancy 2008b).

To allow the thought of the body to open itself to sense, it is necessary to assume the right posture.

Masullo (2003, 67) states that "sense is time, the native emotion of change, the traumatizing irruption of difference, the suffered contingency of the self." In this way, he describes both the disposition toward a condition of continual renewal – which man perceives in his original openness to the world and in the tension that allows for the irruption of difference – and, by reflection, the apprehension of one's own contingency through the Other.

The sense that comes from the encounter with the Other always reveals one's finitude, and finitude determines the horizon of sense that makes time possible. Without this awareness, no transformation would be possible.

Here too lies the connection between sense and *pathicity* (Masullo 2003), which inevitably intertwines the theme of limit with the coming of sense through pain. For this reason, pain – the focus of an important reflection by Natoli (2008a) – is the fundamental human experience.

Inscribed and endured in the body, pain is an original experience – present, possible, and feared – whose occurrence is inevitable. Everyone is exposed to pain, and this, in itself, is both a limit and a cause of suffering. From this perspective, pain becomes the experience of limit in all its forms, allowing the finitude of life, in every manifestation, to be situated within the horizon of death, which is humanity's most painful limit.

For this reason, sense can arise from pain. Man can know only through suffering – when illness and pain suspend the laws of "reason that only reasons" (Rella 1987, 77), which normally govern life and the relation to the world.

Pain is both affliction and revelation: whatever its origin and however it is experienced, it breaks the habitual rhythm of existence, producing a discontinuity sufficient to cast new light on things and to subject human beings to a tension that, when it does not destroy, certainly heightens perception. "On the threshold of pain, if one does not perish, one grows" (Natoli 2008, 73). Moreover, "pain is weight, effort, risk, but also adventure, the investment of one's spiritual energy, and thus a principle of generation and creativity" (Natoli 2008, 114). Profound happiness remains inaccessible to those who are not open to pain, writes Han, echoing Nietzsche's lesson in counterpoint (Han 2021).

Mindful of the lesson of the Greeks, Natoli reminds us that pain produces a kind of knowledge akin to wisdom. The Greeks – and above all the poets – had not failed to see that the best man, the noble, the *agathos*, was he who had been able to pass through pain without losing his mind.

Its prototype was Homer's Odysseus: the man capable of *ex-perire*, of understanding his own condition and reaching beyond contingent reality, and therefore the man of limit, able to envision the future (Mittica 2007). The Greeks imagined a sensitive man, the *polymetis*, gentle and kind, not a mere strategist of survival – a man who possessed a sense of his own finitude and, at the same time, of his potential, one capable of turning toward life and coexistence.

The Greek heroes wept, for they were equal to their pain (Nucci 2013).[4]

Hence the harsh critique of contemporary culture, which relies *en masse* on the logic of a truth about the world elaborated by the technostructure; which seeks to free itself from pain by disguising it as a more superficial malaise, classifying the unease that pervades us – subterranean and diffuse – as anxiety to be soothed or escaped through the various mood tonics made available by the pharmaceutical industry; and, above all, which loses sight of what is positive in the experience of pain – namely, that discontinuity which corresponds to exposure as openness to possibility.

Man suffers, writes Natoli, without being able to have a complete experience of pain. His attention, his care, and his potential "art" are obscured by the dominance of technology.

---

4 On the relationship between suffering and knowledge in ancient Greek culture, see also Curi (2013).

More than that, the technostructure rejects the body and the cumbersome weight of its thought. Natoli observes that "pain is perceived as disturbance, as impediment, as contraction of the possibilities of the I–world relation. In these circumstances, the body is perceived not only as a positive term of distinction with respect to the world but also as a principle of interruption, as an obstacle to processes of interaction" (Natoli 2008, 376).

Ultimately, the technology to which we have entrusted ourselves has resulted in the progressive annihilation of the body. Never before in history, Natoli notes, have the reasons of the body and of the flesh been matters of the spirit, while the understanding of self and world contracts (Natoli 2008, 381).

By deceiving pain, one ultimately deceives both the body and thought, reducing thought to rational intelligence alone. This intelligence is accorded primacy over other forms of intelligence, together with the task of simplifying, translating, flattening, and containing every other mode of understanding – in a word, dominating everything that does not fit into the petty mathematics of the technostructure and its technology. After all, the latter has long since replaced genuine scientific reflection, reducing science itself to mere scientism. Unwittingly, everything that originates from the body is filtered, domesticated, converted, reified, and variously absorbed into the mesh of the technostructure – hidden, if not erased altogether.

Man no longer has access to the limit. The limit is inscribed in his body, yet the human being fails to perceive it.

To reverse this course, it is necessary to reclaim thought, to stand on the side of the exposed body, and to learn to listen to the coming of sense – to understand through synesthesia and through pain – for every experience is an *ac-cadere*: an event and a fall, an ending that allows us to return to the ceaseless movement of our being-body-in-life.

3 On the Edge of the World

The thinking of the body consists in being disposed to the coming of sense, which engages us through the full range of feeling in the moment of contact with something or someone. It is a state of tension: an openness without object, an act of listening, attention, and waiting.

A finite thought, yet open in its striving toward the infinite, arises from the encounter with the Other or with the Thou – an encounter of sensibility that makes it possible to discern the limit that emerges from the presence of the other-than-self and is reflected within us.

The question we must ask ourselves is how to learn to perceive and live this limit, and in what way to make it an art.

Feeling takes form as sense through language. In other words, sensory and affective experience, in all its complexity, lends itself to understanding because it channels into the various forms of language, becoming sense. Every formal construct, whatever the language of human culture, may be regarded as a "deposit of sense." The entire world to which we refer – the culture we have created and continually recreate, as Simmel taught us – is a complex architecture whose elementary units are these forms. We therefore grasp sense within forms, in the articulations of language that crystallize at the moment when sense is apprehended.

In forms, sense manifests itself in various ways – both in explicit, articulable contents and in further contents entrusted to an understanding that goes beyond explanation.

In other words, forms may refer to recognizable meanings, since they can be objects of knowledge through the conventional instruments of the technostructure; yet, they may also contain a non-decodable sense that calls for a deeper understanding.

It is worth making explicit: sense and meaning are not synonymous. While the former may encompass every aspect of our being in the world, reflecting all the tonalities of our experience of living, meanings pertain only to what can be established by convention.

Consequently, if the coming of sense cannot be separated from the experience of forms, it is necessary to learn neither to reduce nor to confine sense, with the awareness that there exists an understanding that goes beyond knowability.

We learn in confusion, writes White (1984), and all the efforts of science to distinguish, define, separate, and reduce are of little avail – and this seems to echo Masullo (2003, 50–51), who affirms that "the comprehensibility of something takes place outside any linguistic-discursive argumentation and any philosophical-specialist thematization."

This does not mean, however, that understanding – which also encompasses feeling – can dispense with form. Quite the opposite.

Without form, that is, outside language, we could not conceive of sense, even in its feeling, in its unsayable dimension. If, therefore, we cannot step beyond the horizon of forms, the point is to reflect once again on the quality of forms and on the technical skill of *homo faber*.

Let us then resume our discussion. If it is through forms that we grasp the sense of our world and continually reformulate it, forms are the most authentic space of our limits.

We may say that form is, in itself, a limit – in the Latin sense of *limen*, which refers to the idea of a threshold: a door slightly opened upon encounter, upon possible relation, and, in any case, upon a beginning. To paraphrase Nancy (2003), form is a limit that unlimits itself.

That is to say, the sense contained within a form is as crystallized in what is meant or conventional as it is open and mobile in what is unsayable yet still intelligible in other ways.

Form is, therefore, the space of limit in which finite thought may wait for and tend toward comprehensibility – a movement sustained by tension and intuition that coincides with attention. Such comprehensibility is destined to coagulate into new forms, configuring new limits – finite chambers with their thresholds.

Form always offers a threshold in which we may find ourselves exposed, in which we may stand as though on the edge of the world.

Now, this threshold may or may not be apprehended by our intelligence.

If we rely on thought confined within calculating and selective rationality, satisfied with closed and infinitely replicable meanings, any form will remain a closed space. More than a limit, it will become a veritable boundary – a wall erected and consecrated to excess. If, however, by engaging the body, we allow ourselves to be touched, it becomes possible to discover ourselves in our exposure to the Other or to the Thou who touches us and whom, perhaps, we also touch. In this contact, predetermined meanings may open up as thresholds for the coming of sense.

This is the posture that allows for the movement of thought that also knows how to feel: thought aware of its own exposure to finitude, capable of understanding by relating itself to an outside.

This is the kind of thought that makes growth and change possible – a thought that arises from the encounter with what is other than itself, that moves in search of sense at the edge of the world, because it knows how to go beyond the meanings stored behind closed doors. In taking new form, it can leave the trace of its passage – open to the passage of new thought and new meanings.

This, too, is technique. Just as form is form: a symbolic construct, a combination of meanings, a fragment of the world.

The point is that if forms were inhabited as thresholds, they would all lend themselves to the making of new forms which, in what escapes convention, would become further thresholds in which thought might stretch itself.

If this were so, with the coming of sense, there might likewise be a coming of the world, marked by the measure of one who has learned to dwell within the limit.

For the Greeks, the technical capacity inherent in the human creature – as compensation for its finitude – was defined by *techne* in its numerous practical declensions:

> The *technai* represent one of the most significant aspects of the Greek experience. When the Greeks questioned the origins of man as a social being and of civil life, they found there the *technai*: at times as elements that diverted man from the simplicity of his origins – more often as aids in the struggle against nature. Moreover, all socially available knowledge consisted in the knowledge of the *technai*. The word *sophia* (wisdom) is attested for the first time in relation to the 'technical' competence of a carpenter – that is, a bearer of *techne* – as if to confirm the primacy of the knowledge of the *technai*. (Gilli 1988, 5)

Techne thus referred to an experience far broader and more complex than that conveyed by the modern concept of technique. It was a principle of creativity and inventiveness – the human capacity to fashion material things, such as a raft, or immaterial ones, such as civil life; to give form, in short, to one's own world. And from this making derived the very possibility of knowledge in every field.

Whether understood as technical capacity in the strict sense or as *virtus poetica*, it was nonetheless *techne*. In the distinction identified by Natoli (2008b, 114–116, 118) when rereading Aristotle, Greek *techne* is *poiesis*, encompassing both "technical creativity," which involves scientific–technological knowledge in the strict sense, and "creative technique," that is, poetic *techne*.

Yet the Greeks maintained an uneasy relationship with it. Throughout the sources of ancient Greek culture, one finds evidence "of a 'defensive' use of the *technai* with respect to the *technai* themselves: a use made up of cautions, limitations, and often of explicit hostility," as Gilli observes (1988, 7). In reconstructing the centrality of this theme, he brings to light the attitude of restraint that Greek society set against technique.[5]

Obsessed with *hybris*, the Greeks feared technical creativity because it heightened humanity's inclination toward domination, drawing both on the strategic quality of human intelligence and on the need to overcome its constitutive weakness.

However, since they also recognized the human capacity to be moved by poetry, they trusted that one could draw on poetic *techne* to explore the

5 Distrust of progress driven by technology and aimed at intervening in nature persisted in both the Roman and medieval worlds, at least until modernity. More generally, innovation was considered dangerous, even to the point of being regarded as "socially harmful" (Bodei 2016).

boundaries of human understanding and learn to contain excess. Thus, alongside the rule used with discernment to straighten a ship's beam, the Greeks set the invisible *metron*, whose reflection could be discerned in *mousike* (Mittica 2015).

The lesson of the Greeks assists us precisely in this intuition: that certain *technai* can be employed to contain others.

To the technique that advances as the creation of a world to be dominated – both feared and inevitable, as is its translation into science – the Greeks, aware of the value of sensibility, which in human beings becomes self-awareness and awareness of being in the world, set alongside the art of the Muses: a different technique, necessary not for survival and domination, but for learning how to exist by taking the limit upon oneself.

The art of the Muses was, moreover, a matter of the body – of thought moving through sensibility within the complexity of feeling, attending to sense, becoming breath, rhythmic form (Mittica 2017).

The Greeks understood perfectly that the Muse's song took shape as sense by holding together the strings of perception, affectivity, and rationality, and that understanding born of synesthesia drew on an intimate, unquantifiable measure preserved in the casket of the unspeakable. They knew that, embraced within the form of song, sense could remain open, and form itself become a threshold – offering a way to perceive both one's own finitude and the measure of the world.

In poetry lay the awareness of touching a kind of knowledge that is a "not-knowing," for mankind cannot surpass the boundaries of the forms and orders it creates; just as it was clear that wisdom could consist only in having learned to dwell within this limit.

The art of the Muses functioned as a counterweight, restraining the human drive toward excessive creative *techne*. To oppose *hybris*, the will to power, and social conflict, poetry was taught and sung everywhere, reminding mortals of the existence of limits – both explicitly, through the speakable dimension of its meanings, and implicitly, through the enigma inscribed in its very form.

The warning was addressed to all. Yet what is most important is that those destined to govern the community had to cultivate this *techne* themselves, learning to listen to the Other, to the Thou, and to themselves, for it alone enabled them to pass through feeling – pain, emotion, passion – and thus to be fully present in communal life.[6]

---

6 At least, this is borne out by the traditions concerning the formation of the earliest political communities. With Plato, the relationship between the city and poetry becomes so uneasy as to lead to the theorization of poets' exclusion from politics. Since the capacity to recog-

This art, in its original features, was inherited over the centuries by many masters of truth, even though, from form to form, the languages in which poetic virtue erupted multiplied, expressing themselves in the great diversity of artistic genres we know today.

The *techne* learned from the Muses thus survives, even as it fragments into the many rooms of the world humanity continues to build. It survives despite having been progressively dismissed, within the vast and intricate yoke of the modern Western division of labor and knowledge, as an instrument of understanding – confined instead to the box of cultural entertainment by a thought that recognizes itself only in the scientism of the technostructure.

What is not lost, Nancy observes (1996), is poetry's most precious quality: its indispensable technical power to give form to the coming of sense, its essential artistry for existence – the natural human aptitude for transformation, of both the external environment and the self, through the creation of a world in which to live, one that, through art, can be traversed and imbued with the sensibility that allows movement within measure.

At this point, the question changes.

It is no longer a matter of determining whether, within the horizon of *techne*, we can find a way out, but whether we are capable of creating a shift away from the culture of the technostructure that has become all-pervasive – so as to reclaim mastery over our own thought and gain access to another order of human capacity for world-making.

Here lies the lesson handed down to us from the past and from the poets, who seem to be the only ones, in the last two centuries, to have preserved the world's most hidden sensibility (Maldiney 2013; Nancy 1997b).

We must reclaim the body, recover the meaning of *techne* that the Greeks identified with poetic virtue, and learn from the art of the Muses to welcome the coming of sense – even when it arises from pain – in order to pass through it.

Sense is present in every form. It is up to us to feel, to stretch ourselves across the threshold of each limit, to look "outside."

To learn from the art of the Muses is to return to attentiveness – to listen, to open ourselves to the unexpected; in a word, to allow ourselves to be touched in order to learn how to touch.

---

nize a man's strength in his capacity to feel no longer exists, not only has the age of heroes definitively come to an end (Nucci 2013), but poetic art can produce nothing but confusion unless duly contained and guided through a *paideia* aimed at controlling the passions. Plato himself, after all – perhaps the greatest poet of antiquity – chose philosophy over tragic composition (Mati 2010).

What matters is to move through sense, in all its feeling, from form to form, rhythmically, so as to grow and to contribute consciously to the *trans-form-action* of the world.

4 Being-in-Common

Revealed by the complex semantics that link it to "the senses," "feeling," "good sense," and "direction" – from affectivity to consciousness, from discernment to practical life – sense demands to be questioned in every form through which we express and construct our being in the world.

There is only one way to question sense, and that is before the Other – whether another human being, a Thou, or any other living being.

Masters of truth, philosophers, and, more generally, all those capable of feeling have never abandoned the awareness of the need to cultivate an art that, engaging all the cognitive resources of the human being, might welcome sense, granting access to self-understanding and to the awareness of one's own finitude – so as to make possible the construction of a world that respects the Other, in the true measure of man.

To experience the coming of sense authentically is what allows one to understand, to grow, and to change – to transform oneself in order to transform. To exist, becoming, within becoming. In a word: to live.

One experiences sense only when it is the body that thinks – that is, when understanding proceeds from the full and integrated sensibility of the sentient human being, when the movement of thought deviates from conventional meanings and places itself at a distance from what remains yet to be thought, becoming, within that space, a thought that gives-to-think (Nancy 2008b).

Unlike the abstract thought of technical rationality, which replicates the finite logic of the system, embodied thinking also feels what lies outside; it understands what it does not comprehend, and it weighs, ponders, and grows heavy, taking upon itself the weight of the Other.

It is, evidently, a matter here of aesthetics joining ethics in the effort to grasp and realize what could count as a *true life* (Jullien 2020).

On the other hand, if – even before taking shape in terms of duty – ethics takes shape in terms of sense (Natoli 2008b, 36–37), one cannot disregard the intelligibility of the felt dimension of sense that comes to us from aesthetics.

> Someone, something, manifests itself, appears, and shakes us to the core, leaving us astonished, disturbed, moved. It does not matter whether it is a work of

> art, a landscape, or a face. What matters is this irruption, into our field of vision, of a reality that surprises and seduces us unexpectedly. (Givone 2003, 13)

A form appears, shaking us deeply.

It happens.

It opens, bringing us to the edge of the world and inviting us into relation with an outside.

Of that something or someone, what surprises and disturbs us is not so much what we had not thought – or could not have thought – as the encounter with mystery itself. It is this reality that seduces us. The indecipherability of mystery engages us, holds us before the Other. Without being unveiled, mystery lends itself to being *com-prehended* – that is, taken with us – emotionally.

Thus, to our knowledge (our ability to explain) of that form – face, landscape, or work of art – is added the indefinable quality that makes it unique and that makes us unique in our understanding of it; a quality that moves us or even frightens us, but that we can *com-prehend* and share only if we accept its unexplainability and its reflection as a mystery of ourselves.

The touch of the Other makes us present, in other words, to the irreducibility of alterity, offering itself as a resource through which we may open ourselves to the coming of sense and to our connection with the Other.

It is thanks to the aesthetic approach that we become familiar not with a mode of thinking bound to the finite, closed sense of form, but with sensibility itself, which allows us to draw upon the affective resources of understanding and to conceive the unexplainability that every form contains. Confrontation with form places us before the limit imposed by the Other, allowing us to come to terms with lack without denying it. This movement beyond finitude is already a configuration of ethics.

Sensitive thought is ethical because, in stretching beyond the threshold of what is already known, it becomes openness, listening, and waiting for the Other, and, by weighing, gives-to-think. In this way, it reveals a being-in-common among "ones" that arises from the finitude that singular existences share-in-common as they relate among "others."[7]

The ethics of finitude (Natoli 2008b, 10) thus becomes attention and respect: it calls man to a shared responsibility for the finitude of sense (Nancy 2003) and to the care of the living, through the shared exposure of every living being to sense.

---

7 Every body is local existence, writes Nancy, clarifying, however, that no such existence is grounded in egoity: the human subject is existentially a body exposed in a world of other bodies, existing by virtue of this being-in-common among "ones" (Nancy 1997a, 2008a).

In these terms, the aesthetic approach also embraces the experience of pain, which becomes compassion, leaving behind the sphere of singularity through the growth of awareness of the finitude of the human condition.

Pain is transformed into a feeling of attentiveness toward the Other that becomes closeness. We might develop a different way of seeing and transforming the world if only we were capable of feeling compassion.

Antonio Prete writes, commenting on certain lines from Leopardi's *Sepulchral Poems*:

> Compassion is swept up by the horizon of finitude in which we all are, in which we breathe. Or, one might say, it leaves the region of singularity – both the observing subject and the figure of the bas-relief – because another, universal, condition now reveals its profile, its laws, its rhythm. *Suffering-with* detaches itself from the relation with the other, with his singularity, and asserts itself as the universal belonging of the living to *physis*, to its perpetual movement of birth and disappearance. Passion is the very breath of life, and that which unites in suffering – the *with* of compassion – is the web of all living beings, the web of the universe. (Prete 2013, 72)

This passage is important not only because it confirms the centrality of the experience of pain, but also because it broadens its scope for being-in-common, highlighting the universal reach of compassion. Compassion leaves the region of singularity because another, universal condition reveals its profile, its laws, and its rhythm.

For Prete, the feeling of compassion concerns the living: it detaches from the relation with the other human being because it asserts itself as the universal belonging of the living to *physis*. In this sense, compassion calls upon humanity itself – before man – to understand the existence of a web that holds together all living beings, implying the promise of human involvement in the care of the living as an indispensable condition within the horizon of constructing one's own world.

The challenge posed by the contemporary age to ethical thought can ultimately be met only if man once again questions sense – exposing himself to mystery, allowing himself to be astonished, welcoming the unexpected and the unfamiliar; letting pain pass through him and take its course; feeling compassion. Man exists only in relation – that is, only if he develops the capacity to project himself into the horizon of true life rather than pseudo-life (Jullien 2020). *Ego cum*, and no longer *ego sum* (Marcantonio 2012).

The question is how to adopt this posture.

It is no coincidence that, in these years of crisis, there has been a proliferation of reflections insisting on rediscovering the value of virtue, particularly the cardinal virtues. Temperance, Fortitude, Justice, and Prudence – all unfold on the horizon of man, who aspires to stand within the distance of what remains yet to be thought (Nancy 2008b), putting into play the capacity to rely on his own resources, both rational and affective, in order to think and cultivate himself in an integrated way, starting from his own exposure. The capable man is the one who is virtuous enough to accept his own fallibility, who possesses an intelligence of limits – the most authentic expression of what it means to be human.

The call addressed to the man who truly wishes to exist is to understand himself – and, even before that, not to lie to himself – by facing the fear of discovering within himself weaknesses, perversions, instincts, and emotions, especially those aspects of himself that he fears and perhaps has repressed.

To enter the ethical dimension, says Crespi (1994, 41), means to confront directly the fear of existence and to assume its anguish, to accept its pain, but without losing oneself. Cultivating virtue serves to *com-prehend* – to take upon oneself the finitude of what one is and what one can be. And with this disposition, one can approach the Other, freeing oneself from the impulse to dominate the living, rediscovering humanity in what we are and realizing what we can be (Natoli 2010b, 9).

Above all, virtue must necessarily be cultivated to free us from the obsession with identity – the reverse side of individualism (Remotti 2017), which has become singularism (Rigotti 2021).

The I, writes Cioran (1968), constitutes a privilege only for those who do not go all the way to the bottom of themselves. Learning to stand before the Other, without reifying it in any form of appropriation, would allow us to discover that it is impossible to confine within a definition who or what the Other is; that one experiences it in the failure to bring it into focus – in an impression, in the air surrounding it, through the energy it seems to emanate, in a handshake, if it is another person. We shall know we have encountered it by the tension it provokes in us (Jullien 2018a).

In this distance, each person may take upon themselves the responsibility of designing a human coexistence founded on solidarity, capable of caring for all forms of life: inventing life by paying attention to the future.

> To invent life means to value it during the time allotted to us and then to relinquish it, to hand it over to others. (Natoli 2010b, 7)

The right posture is adopted by accepting the risk that comes with each person's exposure to alterity, without withdrawing from closeness, compassion, the weight, and the care of the Other. But one must also dare to trust the Other (Natoli 2016).

In his exercises of approaching the Other, Cassano writes:

> There is one gesture, among others, that symbolizes this approach: uncovering one's head – the ritualized imprint of removing the helmet, of revealing oneself, of offering the other the chance to strike while at the same time displaying trust that they will not. [...] Each person remains enclosed within their own code and measures, in the shadow of that code, the gestures of the other [...]. But to set down the helmet is a unilateral act, a decision that seeks to challenge this enclosure, to enact a most delicate form of violence – the attempt to induce the other to do the same. (Cassano 1989, 9)

To choose to uncover oneself is to choose to take a risk and, without seeking to escape one's own exposure, to allow oneself to be touched – inviting the Other to trust and to do likewise. One thus binds oneself, even unilaterally.

Jonas defines this disposition as the *courage of responsibility*: the courage of a person who acknowledges and situates himself within his own precariousness, and who assumes the fear inherent in his exposed condition and transforms it into a duty to act – the responsibility of one who, amid uncertainty, hopes by caring for the Other, for the living.

Responsibility, in this sense, consists of caring for another being once this care is recognized as a moral duty, becoming genuine solicitude when that being's vulnerability is endangered. Fear is always implicit in the fundamental question from which responsible action arises: "what will happen to the Other if I fail to care?" The more troubling the possible answer, the more clearly responsibility emerges (Jonas 1984, 284).

CHAPTER 2

For a Good Use of Law

1 Not Yet Software

It is the capable jurist who responds to the questions of ethics – the one able to construct and order the world – because they know how to attend to sense as it emerges within the affective and cognitive openness of the relationship with the Other.

Perhaps it belongs most originally to the jurist to seek that sense as it opens in the space of alterity, for it is their task to understand and to take on the responsibility of thirdness in safeguarding what transcends the original relationship between the I and the Thou: the common – the axis upon which we build our world.[1] A being-in-common that is third, since it concerns both the reasons of relationship – reasons that go beyond individual interests, in view of a project of human co-existence based on solidarity – and the reasons for committing to the care of other living beings and, more generally, of the natural environment, aimed at limiting the excesses of the unsustainable world of the human species.

Law is the object of this inquiry: a transformative movement, a sensitive experience – feeling, sentiment, and reasoning together – that becomes sense as it takes concrete form in visible and recognizable, though provisional, measures intended to contain the expansion of human individuality.

Whether norms, laws, judgments, or other legal instruments, when formulated or interpreted by a capable jurist, juridical forms are thresholds in which to stretch oneself in order to grasp the reasons for being-in-common. They are forms in which thirdness can arise only through the recognition of alterity: a recognition that implies assuming the weight of the Other. Such responsibility may or may not be reciprocal among human beings; however, it nonetheless entails human responsibility toward the rest of the living, because the living itself is configured as the Other – as that which gives-to-think. They are forms that retain the pathic dimension of their origin, which demands to be appre-

1 On the necessity of the third as a founding principle of law, see the recent reflection by François Ost (2021), who emphasizes the need to re-visit this classical theme in legal studies in order to identify the conditions in which the third function that embodies law emerges, and to recognize the circumstances in which law loses itself – so as, hopefully, to prevent its devitalization.

 | HTTPS://DOI.ORG/10.1163/9789004757714-004

hended also through feeling, beyond that component of sense reducible to mere signification – the exclusive domain of juridical rationality.

To seek the law is therefore the art of the jurist who entrusts themselves to sensitive thought, directing it toward the care of being-in-common.

This practice consists, as Romano (2006) notes, in questioning sense as it can be elicited within the only dimension in which sense can be elicited – that is, "before the Other" – until a form emerges, the most just possible measure, in full awareness that the unquantifiable and the unsaid constitute the inexhaustible truth to which this art draws (Cananzi 2016).

What has just been described is evidently not the conception of law that matured over the course of juridical modernity and that still largely informs contemporary Western legal culture. The principal instrument for defining the orders of today's globalized world – what we identify as law – appears to have little to do with discerning a measure in the service of being-in-common.

Not even the profound crisis affecting every aspect of our lives – indeed, the very survival of the human species – seems sufficient to awaken the world from the "dogmatic slumber" in which it appears immersed, writes Supiot, observing the political, cultural, and economic context dominated by the "no-limits ideology" of globalization and by radical individualism, in which the rule of law has slipped into a form of law shopping subservient to the market economy. The responsibility lies with political institutions at the global level, the French jurist explains, but also with legal science itself, which fails to restore to law its function as a limit against excess (Supiot 2020).

The error lies in continuing to accommodate the process of bureaucratization and its excesses, allowing law to be reduced to a mere mechanism of the infinite multiplication of empty forms (Irti 2007).

For the contemporary jurist, trained by the technical rationality of the legal system to see the world only through predetermined architectures of sense, the risk is that of remaining confined within the autistic logic of juridical representation – cut off from reality – and of using law as a mere mechanical application, thereby losing sight of its purpose.

The consequence, in turn, is a failure to develop the critical distance necessary to question sense, to move away from the enchantments of the many rhetorics of public discourse that, while concealing the dehumanization of the world, legitimize themselves by appealing to the construction of juridical sentiments.

A further risk, from our perspective, is the jurist's habitual marginalization of the resources of sensitive intelligence, tending toward a scientificity founded solely on rationality. We are convinced that the jurist who reduces legal practice to mere mechanics renounces the art of law, thereby forfeiting the future.

Paradoxically (though not surprisingly), it is the future itself – and the role that law and technology play within it – that has become the dominant theme of the salvific narratives employed as *pharmaka* by official and widely disseminated rhetoric.

"We live in the age of rights" is perhaps the most frequent expression linking the representation of law to public discourse in the world we have built. Everywhere, within the boundaries of the "cognitive empire of the West" (Santos 2018), both in common sense and in juridical culture, the illusory idea of a human civilization is accompanied by an equally superficial image of human rights.

Moreover, the capacity to restore sense and historical depth to the reasons behind the affirmation of rights – and to uncover the coercive logic that underlies them – has become ever more fragile. Nor does the bureaucratization of the world take into account the need to confront the complexity of a still incomplete individuation of human rights at the global level, particularly when imagining the shift in perspective and in domains that such a process would require.

For social well-being, provided by the technostructure, the mere foregrounding of rights suffices for the new subjects of our cities to feel themselves their holders or champions. The narrative of fundamental human rights seems to provide the necessary fascination – whether represented as the royal road to liberation from constraints and oppression, to the end of wars or the waging of "just" wars, to the realization of certain models of life, or to the salvation of the planet.

At both the collective and individual levels, behind this enchantment lies not only the affirmation of a culture that seeks to impose the assimilation of its own universal values on a global scale, but also the risk that, in more or less hidden forms, juridical subjectivity may come to coincide ambiguously with unlimited individualism – which, as Elena Pulcini (2009) rightly observes, constitutes the most serious pathology of our age.

The mechanic of law proceeds – defending causes, applying norms, balancing claims – comforted by the legitimacy of his work. Yet they do not inquire further: this is the point.

This is not, of course, to devalue the idea of a possible "good use of human rights" (Supiot 2007), but rather to attempt to crack the taken-for-granted value of that idea by questioning its emblematic orientations and by suggesting the suspicion that, in the assertion of rights, there may develop an excess of egoic affirmation – an excess that might be mistaken for an authentic growth of the person (Natoli 2010b, 62–64).

The jurist attentive to law should not shy away from critique, recognizing in excess one of the many faces of violence (Cotta 1978), whether of the system or of the individual.

But this is not all. We would like to show how, within the discourse of rights, the reasons for fraternity have been lost. If one learns to introduce a distance between one's own judgment and the rhetoric of the rights to liberty and equality, it becomes possible to recognize how the exclusivity of these rights tends to obscure the very foundation of rights themselves – namely, the notion of obligation. As Tommaso Greco (2012) has emphasized, in our contemporary condition, while the catalogue of rights continues to expand, the value of duty – as a fundamental and constitutive dimension of human relations – is increasingly being forgotten. This value, Weil (2024) argues, requires no elaborate explanation: it is realized as attentiveness and respect toward the other human being.

The jurist who questions sense would ask why political thought remains focused on rights rather than duties, when the very fact of the social bond – the foundation of life in common – necessarily entails an authentic relationship with the Other: a conscious choice and a commitment to respond to the other person, taking on the alterity inherent in the relationship, whose presupposition is duty.

A perceptive jurist would also recognize how paradoxical it is that the same logic of asserting rights has been extended even to the protection of the environment – something that should be cared for out of a principle of duty rather than of right, since we ought to be accountable for what is common to every other human being precisely because we are human.

Romano's reflections on the correspondence between law and imputability, anchored in the idea of man, are invaluable in this regard:

> When one names law, one names imputability, referring exclusively to the sphere of man, who speaks in the responsible choice of meaning in words and their coexistent effects and is thus never innocent. To the lexicon of imputability belong intention, decision, plan, and action – dimensions that manifest themselves only in the coexistence of speakers within a language that is communicative discursiveness, not "innocent" but chosen responsibly by free subjects who respond-to. (Romano 2006, 175)

What makes juridicality explicit, writes Bruno Romano, is the assumption of responsibility, which makes a person an I not so much in the sense of identity as in that of imputability – that is, an I who is human to the extent that they take upon themselves the duty to respond-to. It is duty that enables us to stand before the Other, making us accountable for each of our actions, never innocent in the task of safeguarding being-in-common.

Law takes form in the choice of sense embodied in words, within which thirdness must be discernible – in formulas where care and responsible choice become concrete through the discernment of a measure that the jurist must all the more be able to grasp with the *courage of responsibility*.

Alongside the narrative of human rights, the narrative of technological innovation is today, at least in our view, the story that most inspires faith in the human capacity to re-design the future.

After having given us new forms of friendship, communities of ideas, identities and citizenships, and even recipes – all just a click away – on the wave of the successful virtual transposition of each person's affective and cognitive life, technology now turns to saving the environment. The so-called green revolution will be the product of an ill-defined alliance between technology and sustainability.

Thanks to its very immateriality, the cloud serves as its perfect metaphor. Little attention is paid, in the rhetoric of public discourse, to the human, social, and environmental costs of coltan mining in Congo; to the CO_2 emissions generated by the energy consumption of online activity; or to the growing value of the physical infrastructures of the internet – cables and servers – as a form of currency in geopolitical exchange. Technology has no need for critique.

Thus, what should most concern us fails to emerge within mainstream culture – namely, the risk that the ongoing process of dehumanization resulting from the bureaucratization of the world, will find in technological innovation new opportunities for success and an even swifter fulfillment, foreseeable in the growing human will to power, up to and beyond its own self-overcoming. Nor does it occur to many that technological innovation may, in fact, be merely the technical evolution of the same mechanics that have been shaping the human world for centuries – the very mechanics, moreover, blamed for endangering our survival.

More than that, there is no awareness that dehumanization entails precisely the incapacity to evolve; that true change can be generated only by human imagination, since it is the thought of limitation, which "means not only the management and preservation of complexity, but above all choice; it means cyclicality, innovation, and perpetual change in our social life and in its instruments of regulation" (Sterpa 2021, 197).

Ultimately, without a radical reversal of perspective, there can be neither salvation nor future. It is not information technology that provides the means to re-design the world – for it exposes us, if not properly governed, to the excess of a self-destructive passion – but rather a renewed discovery of the human.

The parabola of technological innovation in law unfolds within this very horizon, further burdened by additional factors of crisis: the excessive simplification of language, the tendency to reject any experience of limits, and the "tribalization" of society into homogeneous groups brought about by algorithmic profiling, which heightens the erosion of familiarity with pluralism (Sterpa 2021, 194–196).

After having placed massive confidence in the economic sciences during the latter part of the last century, legal science now entrusts itself to informatics, continuing to align global society with the dominant models of development dictated by the prevailing systems of production and consumption.

The risk is that, in losing the capacity to recognize and give form to limits, jurists themselves will go no further than increasing the efficiency of the legal machine in service to the technostructure – mistakenly persuaded that they are moving toward the future.

For some time now, there have been warnings about the coming to pass of a "legal science without jurists," with the algorithmic revolution viewed as one of the most troubling expressions of the crisis of legal positivism. Legendre, for instance, through the notion of *normative self-service*, identifies the reduction of law to a mere technical moment – a functional instrument of other human phenomena, particularly that of the market – observing how the debacle of law in this direction gives rise to "judicial management" and "normative technocracy."[2] Likewise, Romano (2006, 35) notes the progressive removal of the jurist from legal science and the reduction of that science itself to scientism – the product of the "functional fundamentalism" of bureaucratization – destined to fulfill the "perfect legal nihilism." It has already become a reality, moreover, that artificial intelligence may be substituted for human intelligence even in decision-making processes (Casonato 2020).

The illusion is that new technology will bring about greater technical rationality – perhaps even superior to that of man – as in the case of artificial intelligence. Yet, even while knowing that objectivity is impossible in the human world, the mechanical jurist seems unable to resist the fascination with the idea that precision, objectivity, standardization, and predictability – qualities so often desired for law – might be guaranteed by the calculating reason of a robot. In doing so, they forget that artificial intelligence "is nothing

2 For a reconstruction of Legendre's thought, see the important study by Luisa Avitabile (2004).

but a computing machine. It may well be capable of learning, even of *deep learning*, but it is incapable of experience" (Han 2021).

The reference to mathematical decision-making – that is, to the possibility that an algorithm might define a decision-making process culminating in a choice – reveals, as Sterpa observes (2021, 182), the ambition, if not the presumption, of the jurist to theorize an analogy between mathematics and law, without a clear awareness that the algorithm remains the product of evaluative choices predetermined by its computational parameters.

Even more interesting is what the scholar notes when bringing juridical science closer to the other sciences of posthumanism:

> One aims to replace the human (acting and thinking) with a non-human (acting and thinking) after having simplified and trivialized it – that is, rendered it transferable from the body to the machine. Law, for its part, is fascinated by this potential dehumanization, insofar as it would represent the perfection of its capacity to act in fulfilling the very function for which it was created: to make the consequences of human action predictable.
>
> The attraction that law feels toward mathematics stems from the fact that contemporary humanity remains seduced by the attempt to overcome "the lack" inherent in its very nature – in its corporeality and finitude, as well as in the presence of the other. (Sterpa 2021, 192–193)

By highlighting the replacement of the human with the non-human – transposing the human from body to machine after simplifying and trivializing it – Sterpa points, on the one hand, to the increase in technical rationality and legal formalization functionally linked to the management of the world's growing complexity, and, on the other, to the abandonment of affective and cognitive expressions that do not lend themselves to mechanical prediction through mathematical processes. The dehumanization of law emerges in the passage from body to machine, through the erasure of what in man remains irreducible to computational language, along with the consequent impoverishment of our understanding of the living.

It is a dead end, which moreover nullifies the very hope of remedying the pain arising from the wound of one's original exposure – a wound that Sterpa recognizes at the heart of humanity's fascination with mathematics. A double wound: to the finitude of one's being, inscribed in one's body – the limit of the self-suggested by the presence of the Other – is added the impossibility of reducing the Other to oneself, leaving it to remain in its alterity. It is a painful, unresolved irreducibility that drives the urge toward expansion and domination under the sign of excess.

The jurist who questions sense would not succumb to the enchantment of the future promised by the technostructure. Such a jurist would use technology insofar as it is useful, aware that law, when exposed to computerization, may err through excessive simplification or excessive complication; that the reduction or multiplication of forms and procedures is not, in itself, either negative or positive, but may lead to error and, consequently, to injustice.

The jurist who is not yet software might understand that the fallibility of the legal process is "its greatest virtue, and not paradoxically" (Ferrari 2020); that the problem does not lie in whether or not legal technique should incorporate the instruments of new information technology, but in understanding the extent to which mechanical intervention can provide support without becoming distortive – reflecting, in an informed and interdisciplinary way, on the implications entailed by the contamination of different kinds of knowledge and language in the face of the technologization of the world (Garapon and Lasségue 2018).

Here, too, the point is not the condemnation of technology but that of false representations.

The future should not be entrusted to technology but to human intelligence – an intelligence that does not deny the thinking of the body: thought that knows its limits; finite thought, because it cannot abstract itself from the physicality of one's own body and that of the Other; sensitive thought, that feels the presence of the Other and takes on its weight; thought of alterity, that makes distance possible, preventing the assimilation of the Other into the Self; thought that does not deny the experience of pain; and finally – though not least – thought that is juridical sentiment, because it cares for the thirdness of being-in-common.

To counter the dehumanization of law, the jurist who is not yet software should rediscover – to put it succinctly – an art that unites "technical creativity" and "creative technique," that is, technical rationality and poetic virtue, so that the original sense of law is not lost and norms may order the world effectively as expressions of true life within an imaginative and shared vision of the common.

In this perspective, it is worth repeating that, more than law itself, what comes into play is duty, for the pursuit of law requires responsibility and attentiveness, so that within juridical form the limit embodied in being-in-common may become manifest – a limit whose measure is entrusted to the discernment of the jurist-as-artist, who knows how to question sense.

2 The Juridical, Justice, and Law

If we wish to restore law to the horizon of the search for sense, we must move away from the many definitions that reduce it to an agglomeration of norms, apparatuses, and procedures. Before making it an object or a tool, we must think of law as an experience – an existential experience that proceeds from sensibility.

Before the Other, the human being who learns to exist as a sentient body – encountering the Other, touching and being touched – is already a jurist the moment they entrust themselves to a mode of thought capable of taking upon itself the weight of the Other: a thought that gives-to-think. The juridical, as we have said, implies the assumption of responsibility: the free choice, as Romano (2006) affirms, of one who takes upon themselves the commitment to being-in-common, to existing as co-existing.

To recognize alterity is juridical sentiment (Savona 2005), just as it is an affective act to be accountable for the common before every other human being, and – as a human being – before the living; and it is sentiment because the attentiveness implied by this recognition calls upon both the affective and cognitive resources of human intelligence. The jurist who would be capable must learn the art of sensitive thought, for only through such attentiveness, with all one's energies, can juridical sense arise – the only kind capable of enabling the care of the third.

To question feeling in relation to law has long ceased to be heresy. The need to investigate the relationship between law and the passions and emotions is increasingly recognized,[3] as is the growing interest in developing an integrated reflection on the relation between law and the senses.[4]

3 As is well known, the debate that began in the 1990s (see Bandes 1999) has been significantly enriched by research conducted in the field of neuroscience and is now wide-ranging and multi-faceted in legal studies as well. Here, specific reference is made to the reflections of Rouland (2005) and Ost (2018) on the possibility of developing a general theory of legal passions, while on the long, close, and complex historical connection between law, reason, and emotion within the traditions of philosophy and justice, see Sellers (2017) and West (2015). For a *paideia* of the passions, from a broader perspective, see Pulcini (2020).

4 The development of this line of inquiry has been so significant that it has led scholars to speak of a "sensory turn" in legal studies. A well-documented reconstruction of the law's sensory turn is provided by Hamilton *et al.* (2017). The volume is the outcome of a joint research project between the Center for Sensory Studies at Concordia University – co-directed by David Howes – and the Canadian Initiative in Law, Culture, and Humanities at Carleton University (LCH), directed by Sheryl Hamilton. It offers both a mapping of studies beginning in the 1990s (see, in particular, Bently and Flynn 1996; Hibbitts 1992) and an attempt to chart a "cartography" of sensing law, adopting a conception not limited to the five senses (Grabham 2009), aimed at understanding the multisensory way in which

From this development arises, more generally, the theoretical advancement of a legal aesthetics – as a possible sensitive approach to the understanding of law – alongside the Law and Humanities methodology, which offers a valuable practical application in the educational dimension of legal training.[5]

As several scholars have observed, the task is to consider law within its sensory context, developing a multisensory notion of the *lawscape*, or "juridical landscape":

> Law is thus found not only in judicial decisions, legislation, or contracts, but also in the smell of trees burning in the Amazonian forest, in the flavor of the tomatoes or vegetables we eat, in the nursery rhymes and protest songs we hear, or in the urban landscapes we inhabit, where issues as diverse as housing, spatial segregation or street art have a direct legal component. In addition, legal conflicts often have an emotional dimension, but judicial proceedings, governed by strict rules and rituals, control and regulate the display of affect and emotion in the courtroom. (Branco and Nitrato Izzo 2017, 51)

It is no coincidence that some have linked the notion of space to that of atmosphere (Philippopoulos-Mihalopoulos 2013), integrating the more traditional cognitive approach of legal science with a synesthetic one (Marusek 2020).

What is often criticized in legal scholarship – which still struggles to move beyond technicism and formalism – is the prevailing conviction that rationality can and must dominate feeling. This conviction, accompanied by an exclusively negative assessment of the resources of sensibility, persuades legal practitioners that they can remain immune to feeling, thanks first to their training (beginning with their *forma mentis*) and later through the formal and informal rituals of professional practice perpetuated by the mechanics of the system.

And yet innumerable traces of feeling remain impressed in juridical forms. Indeed, while legal science places its faith in the rational capacity to cool emotions and passions – to distance sensations in order to formulate rational and objective norms – juridical forms, like shells embedded in language, are

---

law operates and how law and the senses are mutually constitutive. For a broader and more up-to-date overview, see Antaki (2019); Branco and Nitrato Izzo (2017); Franca-Filho (2014); Howes (2013; 2019); Mandic *et al.* (2015); Nirta *et al.* (2020); Pavoni *et al.* (2018a; 2018b).

5 For a precise delineation of these studies in their historical perspective and international context, see Zeidler (2020). It is also worth emphasizing the long-standing debate on legal aesthetic within Italian legal philosophy, which seeks to link, on the one hand, the methodology of Law and Humanities with legal education and practice, and, on the other, the aesthetics of law with ethics (Cananzi 2013, 2016, 2017a; Condello and Heritier 2021; Heritier 2012, 2013; Messner 2018; Mittica 2021).

imbued with metaphors, images, feelings, and passions that the jurist, in identifying them, believes they can govern and employ (after all, the invention of *fictio iuris* belongs to the jurist), yet without truly grasping their full significance. In other words, the jurist trained solely in the mechanics of the system fails to perceive in language the thresholds that present themselves as opportunities to question the reality of what is unsaid and only alluded to (Galgano 2010).

This reality, it bears repeating, should not be understood in terms of possible objectivity but as real, embodied sense – something that transcends the analytical dimension of formal expression, of definitions or explanations – and whose comprehensibility can be grasped only by a mode of thought capable of moving beyond the conventional meanings of form, to which the jurist must turn in order to question sense and discern, through that form, a measure.

The emotional return of sensations is another matter – one that should not be avoided, whatever form these sensations may take, for they open further thresholds of understanding (LeBaron 2020). Even though this may entail exposure to feelings that could influence judgment – positively or negatively, depending on each person's inner disposition – the point is to learn how to govern one's sensibility with balance, translating passions into resources.

The capable jurist understands, in other words, that prudent judgment requires moderating feeling without, however, denying sensitive understanding – indeed, by drawing upon it – while remaining fully aware that rationality, even when supported by accurate and technical knowledge of the law, is not the surest way to shield oneself from the influence of emotions (Forza, Menegon and Rumiati 2017). Yet this is no easy task, and there are no instruction manuals. The only guidance is to cultivate within oneself a disposition of sensitive openness, so as to adopt a posture attuned to the coming of sense.

In other words, it means keeping the senses awake – paying attention to what is revealed through smells and tastes, sounds and noises, touch rather than sight alone. How much influence, for example, might it have in a trial if hearings are held in a bunker courtroom, under neon lights, before defendants confined in cages? In what ways does the architecture of the spaces in which law unfolds matter? Can this condition of potential discomfort affect the mental processes involved in judgment (Nitrato Izzo 2017)?

Sensitive knowledge assists, on the one hand, in understanding the real landscape of law, enabling the jurist to intervene in ways more closely attuned to concrete situations; on the other, it nourishes imagination, awakening the potential to envision a new landscape by drawing upon emotional openness to conceive what is possible.

The idea is that law, arising from the complex experience of the sentient body, is a form of sense shaped by synesthesia, in the same terms discussed earlier (see above, 13-17) – as a kind of feeling that unites sensory perception, emotion, and rationality. Moreover, this allows us to relate the idea of law as the movement of sensitive thought to that expressed by the notion of juridical sentiment, which originates in the primordial experience of the Other and in the need to regulate one's exposure to the Other, opposing the measure of being-in-common to the excess of individual predominance. In this sense, it seems possible to embrace the profound connection that Masciandaro (2018) identifies between poetry and law.

A corollary of our thesis on law is that, in order to find the measure needed at any given moment for the care of being-in-common, one must turn to a form of thought that – by embracing its own emotional, passionate, and sensitive dimensions – knows how to use and to limit rationality intelligently, while also recognizing its dangerous potential to become, when employed to conceal pain or death, a cold passion bent toward excess: a tool for strategies of domination, animated by reason, certainly, but by a destructive form of reason. For the reason of law is not a reason that merely reasons.

A further corollary is that the very practice of this kind of thinking is, in its origins, juridical, for it avoids the domination of one feeling over another, striving instead to hold together, to moderate, to temper. It is not by chance – and it is more than a mere suggestion, as we shall soon see – that temperance, an attitude that can be cultivated only through sensitive thought, is, among the cardinal virtues, the one most closely associated with prudence, the virtue lying at the very roots of the juridical (Bodei *et al.* 2017).

From the same root of law thus conceived arises the sentiment of justice. Justice too implies the dutiful feeling of responding-to from the perspective of responsibility toward the *alterum* understood as thirdness (Pulcini 2009, 224).

However, within the flow of law, the movement of justice proceeds through requests and responses: it is invoked, it is given, it is done. It follows that, before the Other, in relation to the Other, justice – guided, like law, by attentiveness – is a tension within the search for sense, aimed at identifying concrete actions capable of realizing the good for the Other, a good that can be *com-prehended* only by taking upon oneself even that which cannot be explained: the irreducibility of the Other's alterity.

The person who seeks to be just must stretch themselves within this distance, in respect for both self and Other – even within what is lacking – to find the measure, that is, the course of action that can respond to the demand for justice. Such a person is the capable jurist, for the measure found within the limit of irreducible alterity is both the foundation and the form of law.

A sense of responsibility and duty are not the only sentiments that guide the response to the Other who calls for justice. The unfolding of justice is animated by the understanding of the pain of the Other who is in a condition of suffering. It may be the pain of another human being who experiences a sense of injustice (Greco 2005), or the suffering of other living beings – of the natural environment – which we, as human beings, directly feel to be unjust. The point is to allow pain to pass through us so that we may belong to ourselves and recognize ourselves as human among other living beings within the living whole.

In this, suffering holds the power to transform – to dispose us to openness and to the coming of sense that creates closeness among men, presence, and care toward the living Other. And this does not necessarily mean referring to empathy, a notion far too overused and misunderstood (Pinotti 2011). It is naïve to hope to "feel in the same way" or to "put oneself in the Other's shoes," and indeed, either may become dangerous when empathy is associated with law (Massaro 1989).

Closeness to the suffering Other is to be understood, rather, as compassion: love for the Other, suffering with the Other, without allowing the singularity of feeling – each person being themselves and feeling in their own way – to lapse into egoism or pity.

Let us return once more, on this point, to Prete (2013), in order to grasp fully the link between compassion and justice, beginning with the exclusion of false compassion:

> Compassion is [...] a rare feeling. For rare is the experience in which another's pain truly becomes one's own. The word "compassion" often covers, like a comforting veil, a kind of feeling in which attention to the other, to their pain, is accompanied by a certain self-satisfaction of the compassionate subject, a silent confirmation of their own goodness of heart. (Prete 2013, 9)

Authentic compassion, by contrast, is a sentiment that reconnects us to life in its entirety, for it enables closeness to the Other and care for the Other, with attention to thirdness and respect for the distance opened by alterity. Here lies its common matrix with justice, and the substance of a notion that, largely discredited in the Western philosophical tradition, has nonetheless survived – once again – thanks to poets:

> Writers and artists have, instead, represented the degrees and forms of compassion's manifestation – its language, its gestures, its cognitive tension. They have shown the great scene in which compassion takes form: the community of the living, the finitude that unites within the same circle all living beings, human and animal alike, each with the singularity of their bodies, desires, and wounds.

> The literary, artistic, and theatrical representation of compassion is the unbroken narration of a presence – that of the other, of their face, of their unfathomable depths. A presence that sustains the very identity of the one who gazes. And it stirs a feeling that flows from the subject back toward the feeling of the other. It becomes, finally, the recognition of the bond that runs among all beings. Within the horizon of this shared belonging, the pain of the other calls not for indifference but for proximity. (Prete 2013, 10–11)

The proximity to the Other that compassion entails engages, as in justice, the interiority of each person: one's own relationship to pain, a gathering of oneself within oneself that can then draw breath and make space for a new kind of listening (Prete 2016, 45–46). It is not a love that imposes itself or attracts the Other by objectifying them according to one's own idea of the good; rather, compassion moves within the terrain of an intimacy that opens to relationship with another human being (Jullien 2013) and to the recognition of the bond that connects all beings within the horizon of a shared belonging (Prete 2013, 11).

In this landscape, respect for distance translates into the capacity to draw near to the Other – to feel them, to listen to them in what is silent, to suffer with them in their pain – choosing to limit oneself (Mittica 2012). "Silence is not the nothingness of thinking-speaking, but the responsible preparation of the words to be uttered; it reorients the deferral-of-meaning of words already spoken" (Romano 2006, 36). Justice arises from this disposition to inner attentiveness, opened toward the Other (Constable 2005).

It falls to the capable jurist to give measure to all that is felt – to define, in a form, a concrete course of action. In this way, one responds to the call. The discernment of measure is an *activity-for*, as Cotta (1978) writes, bearing in mind that justice will exist only once it has existed (Resta 2009) – that is, if and when the measure identified has healed the wound for which it was invoked.

Justice happens. Only if and after it has happened can we understand that justice has been done – when the measure has been found, or has found us.

Justice will surprise us, in wonder and in feeling.

Not because of the explanation we have received, but because we will feel it as right. We will feel that peace has been made, that everything has returned to measure, that the solution is fitting, because new reasons have found their place within us.

The event of justice triggers an opening that transcends the value of the expressed solution itself. Thus, in occurring, justice already places itself beyond the very form through which it has taken place, becoming the further possibility of a better relationship with the Other through the emotional resonance that this opening has produced. In this sense, justice is subversive: it proceeds from creative imagination.

Law and justice are movements within the same flow of sense. Juridical sense takes form in juridical expressions – norms or judgments – in which the measures discerned by the jurist are crystallized to realize the good of being-in-common. Law consists of these forms: it is instituted thirdness, the formal expression of law that enacts the reasons of thirdness (Ost 2021). In other words, law is sense made concrete in the language used to express juridical forms.

Juridical forms are rhythmic – forms in movement, according to the Greek notion of *rhythmos* (Maldiney 2013; Mittica 2017). However formulated, they retain the complexity of feeling that keeps them open to the coming of sense. They are not completed forms, resolved once and for all. As Satta writes (1994) the juridical form has the distinctive quality of being full and infinite, capable of giving expression to experience and to its free movement.[6] Essential in structure for law, it presents itself as a threshold within a liminal space where the interpreter, employing sensitive thought, can venture outward and, in awareness of limits, discern the most just measure for the concrete situation.

From forms proceed new forms. Like every form of human culture, juridical forms, too, are animated by a formative power that ceases only when the possibility of taking into account what is inexplicable – yet still comprehensible in other ways – is abandoned (see above, 18). Each time the sense contained within them is questioned by the legal interpreter in order to regulate a segment of our world, the form transforms, yielding new and varied nuances.

Only the juridical form that remains on paper, without application, has come to an end.

It follows that juridical sentiment is a transformative movement affecting not only juridical forms themselves but also the sensibility of the jurist who seeks to question sense by activating all the cognitive resources of feeling.

The Juridical, Justice, and Law. In authentic openness to the Other, the capable jurist takes up the questions of ethics. Within the limit of the finitude of the I – which does not allow one to grasp sense as such, but only, from moment to moment, the sense of something, in the awareness of a condition

6 The theme of form in relation to law – and in open critique of legal formalism – has been the subject of an important debate in Italian scholarship. For an overview, see the significant contributions collected in Avitabile (2011).

that obliges one to choose (Romano 2012) – this jurist bears responsibility for discerning the reasons and the care of being-in-common.

3 Fossils

From every age, memories resurface like fossils in the history of Western culture, bearing witness to the enduring idea of a form of law akin to feeling, in the sense explored thus far. These recollections bring to light the original kinship between law and poetic art, between aesthetics and ethics, between sensitive knowledge, the orientation toward the good, and the capacity to envision the future. This unearthing is fascinating – it awakens wonder and offers consolation.

3.1 *Arete*

Tracing back through the semantics of the term that, in ancient Greek, denotes virtue – *arete* – we learn that the word, which in the Homeric culture of honor designates the most complete heroic virtue (Adkins 1972), is also the name of the wife of Alcinous, king of the Phaeacians, in the *Odyssey*. This fact is significant for at least two reasons.

First, the narrative's portrayal of Phaeacian society as a model of a perfectly ordered and peaceful community – one toward which humanity should aspire – bears witness to a shift in values within the culture of honor: from the exaltation of warrior virtues to the recognition of heroism in those capable of imagining and building a life of peace, such as that to which the poem's protagonist is destined.

The second consideration concerns more closely the special relationship between Queen Arete and Odysseus. In this relationship, a perfect form of approach to the Other is realized. Odysseus, the unwanted stranger, clasps the knees of the king's wife before the council of nobles in an act of supplication, seeking help and support for his journey home. Man to woman, stranger to stranger.

In this respect, the advice Nausicaa gives to Odysseus is particularly interesting (Od. 6.289–315):

> Stranger, do thou quickly hearken to my words, that with all speed
> thou mayest win from my father an escort and a return to thy land.
> [...] But when the house and the court enclose thee,

> pass quickly through the great hall, till thou comest
> to my mother, who sits at the hearth in the light of the fire,
> spinning the purple yarn, a wonder to behold,
> leaning against a pillar, and her handmaids sit behind her.
> There, too, leaning against the selfsame pillar, is set the throne of my father,
> whereon he sits and quaffs his wine, like unto an immortal.
> Him pass thou by, and cast thy hands about my mother's knees,
> that thou mayest quickly see with rejoicing the day of thy return,
> though thou art come from never so far.
> If in her sight thou dost win favour,
> then there is hope that thou wilt see thy friends, and return
> to thy well-built house and unto thy native land.

Likewise, it is also revealing to observe how Odysseus presents himself to the queen (Od. 7.139–152):

> He passed quickly over the threshold into the house.
> There he found the leaders and counsellors of the Phaeacians
> pouring libations from their cups to the keen-sighted Argeiphontes,
> to whom they were wont to pour the wine last of all,
> [when they were minded to go to their rest.
> But the much-enduring goodly Odysseus went through the hall,
> wrapped in the thick mist which Athena had shed about him,
> till he came to Arete and to Alcinous the king.
> About the knees of Arete Odysseus cast his hands,
> and straightway the wondrous mist melted from him,
> and a hush fell upon all that were in the room at sight of the man,
> and they marvelled as they looked upon him. But Odysseus made his prayer:
> "Arete, daughter of godlike Rhexenor,
> to thy husband and to thy knees am I come after many toils,
> – aye and to these banqueters, to whom may the gods grant happiness
> in life, and may each of them hand down to his children
> the wealth in his halls, and the dues of honor which the people have given him.
> But for me do ye speed my sending, that I may come to my native land,
> and that quickly; for long time have I been suffering woes far from my friends."

Added to the mystery of this encounter is the power Arete exercises over the aristoi of Scheria with acknowledged authority – feminine power in the face of masculine power within a patriarchal society.

Nausicaa describes her mother as an honored woman (Od. 7.66–774):

> Arete. Her Alcinous made his wife,
> and honored her as no other woman on earth is honored,
> of all those who in these days direct their households in subjection
> [to their husbands;
> so heartily is she honored, and has ever been,
> by her children and by Alcinous himself
> and by the people, who look upon her as upon a goddess,
> and greet her as she goes through the city.
> For she of herself is no wise lacking in good understanding,
> and for those whom she wishes – even men – she settles disputes.[7]

Moreover, within the alterity through which Arete and Odysseus recognize one another, there opens a form of absolute hospitality that requires no reciprocity (Mittica 2007, 34–35). Through the virtue embodied by Arete, the Phaeacians and the king of Ithaca discover an original reciprocity among human beings, rooted in *ethos* even before taking juridical form – that is, before becoming the customary pact of alliance sealed by reciprocal gifts between host and guest.

This is what the law of hospitality – first and foremost, the duty to assist life – reminds us of, and what makes possible the hope of a future. A visible sign of this is the linen sheet given by Arete to Odysseus, in which, during his voyage home to Ithaca, he is wrapped "an unawakening sleep, most sweet, and most like to death" (Od. 13.80), as though, by accompanying the hero toward a new rebirth Arete could bestow the gift of time (Derrida 1991).

In the Homeric account, virtue is thus at the origin of the bond of solidarity between guests, as an attitude that turns the encounter with the Other into a possibility of communion. The virtue that Arete shares with Odysseus is the art that makes possible the safeguarding of thirdness and that finds expression in the rules of hospitable law conveyed through the poetry of the *aoidoi*.

A trace of the kinship between virtue and art also remains in the Latin language, where *arete* – as Natoli observes (2010b, 20) – shares the root *ar* with the term *ars*, suggesting at least the idea that the technical art of the *homo faber* already carries within itself the seed of a sensibility closer to poetic *techne* and its forms, through which the meaning of the original *arete* and its juridical import are transmitted.

The most explicit link between virtue and law – and, at the same time, the most revealing of the original intertwining of aesthetics and ethics, that is, of poetry and law – appears in the forms of the two cardinal virtues of prudence

---

7 Unlike the translation adopted here by A. T. Murray, the rendering of Od. 7.74 is my own.

and temperance, whose rule expressly requires a mode of thought capable of feeling.

According to its etymological root, prudence derives from the Latin *prudentem*, accusative of *prudens*, itself a contraction of *providens*, the present participle of *providere*. The *prudens* is therefore the *pro-videns*: the one who sees ahead, from afar; the one who, in foreseeing the outcome of actions, also takes care to provide – that is, to take the necessary precautions to avoid, or at least to contain, their possible negative effects.

Prudence is the deliberative virtue *par excellence*, which places those who practice it in a position not only to discern good from evil but also to prepare for the future by drawing upon the lessons of the past. It is thus a powerful antidote to rash action, fanaticism, and arbitrariness (Bodei *et al.* 2017, 5).

Within the semantics of *prudentia* lies the highest expression of practical wisdom oriented toward the future. Prudence is the virtue that serves decision. To reduce its meaning to the modern sense of caution would be highly misleading, betraying its deepest nature as a force animated by the courage to determine events. What characterizes it, rather, is the disposition to extend evaluation across a time better understood as duration: a time of patience, capable of grasping the best possible decision – one discerned through the exercise of experience but also of imagination.

A prudent decision arises from the sensitive capacity to comprehend the complexity of situations. It is not so much the eye – the *videns* – that defines it, as the time of the *providens*: a time of attentiveness, the time that must be allowed, endured, and attended to in order to understand.

Prudence is a disposition toward foresight – toward discerning future possibilities and risks – drawing strength from experience inherited from the past. It is the capacity to comprehend, within the present, both past and future. As with Hesiod's king-judge, who can contemplate like a poet "things that are and that shall be and that were aforetime" (*Theogony* 38), the *providens*, faced with the present question before him, allows his thought to stretch forward, to reach ahead, and – within the limits of that reaching – to expose itself to mystery, to the Other, to the imagination of the future.

Like a charioteer leading and steering the other virtues – each a "hinge" of human co-existence – *prudentia* shows a special kinship with *temperantia*. The latter serves prudence, above all, because it is associated with inner formation. It is a quality that enables the one who possesses it to understand differing – if not opposing – demands, through the balance achieved within the self. In self-awareness, the temperate person is the one who knows how to sense the temperature of situations and, by virtue of their own measure, to discern the measure of conduct.

In the deepest layers of our culture, this particular bond between virtue and sensory perception is revealed by the myth of the Horae, which embodies the *mimesis* between the natural rhythms of the seasons and the juridical forms of political co-existence.

The three Horae, also known as the Seasons and destined to watch over the natural order, are likewise connected to the life of human communities. The mythical narrative suggests the reasons for this investiture, which can be traced to their genealogy: they were born of the union between Zeus and Themis – the former, father of the gods of the new divine order; the latter, goddess of the law of the universe and the only one among the first-generation deities to sit upon Olympus. Yet this *mimesis* is fulfilled above all in the testimonies of Hesiod and Solon, who identify the Horae as *Eunomia*, *Dike*, and *Eirene* – the goddesses devoted to the care of communal life through good laws, justice, and peace.

> Next he [Zeus] married bright Themis who bore the Horae (Hours),
> and Eunomia (Order), Dike (Justice), and blooming Eirene (Peace),
> who mind the works of mortal men; (*Theogony* 901–903)

It is therefore to poetry that the task is given of revealing the most complex and original sense of the juridical – of tracing it back to a sensibility for proportion, prudence, and measure, which cannot be separated from the law that governs the universe, from the natural order.

As Hesiod reveals, poetic song originally played a formative role in the daily life of political communities, setting out a model of good government grounded in a strong bond between *mousike* and sovereignty. Indeed, it is the Muses who instruct the song of kings:

> These things, then, the Muses sang who dwell on Olympus,
> nine daughters begotten by great Zeus,
> Cleio and Euterpe, Thaleia, Melpomene
> and Terpsichore, and Erato and Polyhymnia and Urania
> and Calliope, who is the chiefest of them all,
> for she attends on worshipful princes:
> whomsoever of heaven-nourished princes the daughters
> of great Zeus honour, and behold him at his birth,
> they pour sweet dew upon his tongue,
> and from his lips flow gracious words.
> All the people look towards him while he settles causes
> with true judgements: and he, speaking surely,

> would soon make wise end even of a great quarrel;
> for therefore are there princes wise in heart, because when the people
> are being misguided in their assembly, they set right the matter
> again with ease, persuading them with gentle words.
> And when he passes through a gathering, they greet him as a god
> with gentle reverence, and he is conspicuous amongst the assembled:
> such is the holy gift of the Muses to men. (*Theogony* 75–93)

There is a rhythm to be grasped, the poets seem to remind us, if one aims at good governance – a rhythm that cannot be detached from the breath of the earth, from the pulse of the living, of which human beings and their world are a part, and whose key of access is sensibility. The person who governs the city must be like the musician who, by listening to the living, questions sense and finds the forms through which human co-existence may be regulated with moderation and respect for the Other.

The strongest historical evidence of this is provided by Solon, as attested by the fragments of his poetic corpus. Thanks to these sources, we have the rare opportunity to observe a first-hand interpretation of the link between *mousike* and lawgiving, articulated by a figure who embodied the dual role of poet and *nomothete*. For Solon, sapience coincides with wisdom, and poetry stands as the form best suited to its revelation. But caution is required. No knowledge can ever be complete, and wisdom lies in the awareness that human beings can act only within a limit. Only poetry can express this "truth." Solon therefore insists on the impossibility of knowledge except as "measure" (*metron*), noting how difficult it is to identify each specific measure, but also emphasizing how necessary this task is, since Measure establishes the natural order of things.

In fragment 13 W., 51–52, Solon (via Lewis 2006) sings that *dike*, shrouded in silence, knows the things that are and those that were. In these verses, he draws on a formula borrowed from *Theogony* (32, 38), where Hesiod evokes the king providens. Solon deliberately sings of the silence of justice, for he is convinced that the truth of justice – unsayable in words and immeasurable – can be revealed only through song (Mittica 2015, 22–27).

Here we reproduce only one fragment, which explicitly sets out the nature of *eunomia* and its close relationship with prudence:

> These things my heart prompts me to teach the Athenians:
> how Lawlessness (*Dysnomia*) brings the worst evils to the city, and
> Lawfulness (*Eunomia*) manifests good order
> [and everything proper,

and often puts fetters on the evil-doers.
It smoothes what is rough; quells anger, dims hubris
and shrivels the flowering bud of arrogant destruction.
It straightens crooked judgments, calms
overbearing deeds, stops the deeds of civil strife,
and stops the anger of grievous conflict.
It is by this that all things to men
[are proper and prudent (*pinuta*) thoughts.[8]
(Solon, 4 W., 30–39, via Lewis 2006)

Prudence and temperance. Seasons and juridical forms. Laws as fruits. If prudence finds its center in the capacity to see through time, temperance finds its own in the capacity to grasp rhythm – as the transformative movement of the living, which, like the earth and its fruits, shapes the forms that regulate human relationships.

Thus, prudence's foresight and temperance's rhythmic disposition emerge as necessary attributes for stretching oneself within limits and for striving to mediate among different demands – to temper, indeed, the harshness of opposing positions, in accordance with the common meaning traditionally attributed to this virtue in broader culture. And within this same tension, to share responsibility for the care of the living.

3.2 *Aidos*

The encounter with the Other reveals alterity as reflected both in the Other as such – who resists our tendency to reduce them to ourselves, to our representations, interpretive categories, prejudices, appetites, and self-interest – and in the Other that each of us is to ourselves: that part of us which eludes our grasp, the missing part that exposes us and fuels our obsession with domination.

Entirely different from the reaction to negative judgment (including self-inflicted judgment) that characterizes shame, modesty (*aidos*) takes the form of reserve and restraint, realized in the resistance one human being offers to another by keeping them precisely at a distance. It is a defense against objectification, against the appropriation that the Other enacts – even uncon-

8 With respect to the translation adopted here, by John D. Lewis (2006), the exact terms found in the source text have been added in parentheses in order to show the effective correspondence between the English text and the Greek. The translation of verse 39 of the fragment, however, is my own, intended to convey the meaning of "prudent" that is proper to the semantics of *pinute* and of the adjective *pinutos*, here employed in its Homeric usage and recurrent in the language of Solon.

sciously – when they are unable to acknowledge the irreducibility of the alterity made present in the encounter.

Modesty is, therefore, a form of withdrawal within relation – so that an openness, a tension toward the Other can be maintained without this implying a denial of relationship. On the contrary, it becomes a resource for it, since it entails mutual awareness and respect (Cotta 1978, 125–127; Guardini 1980; Orazi 2020). Only within the distance opened by alterity is possible to respect the Other and to assume responsibility for the Other as a duty guided by the sentiment of compassion, within the horizon of being-in-common.

Modesty is a quality that prepares us for the coming of sense, opening us to the liminal space of attending to the juridical dimension, reinforcing the idea of law as a movement that arises from sensitive thought – that is, as sense shaped by synesthesia, apprehended through every perception stirred by the presence of the Other. It is no coincidence that this notion has returned to question us about the human quality of moderation that emerges in the presence of alterity, and its deep connection with law.

In this direction, a particularly insightful path has been traced in the study of modesty in the thought of Vico.[9]

For the Neapolitan philosopher, modesty is what distinguishes human beings from other animal species, making them conscious, thinking creatures. The distinctively juridical quality that characterizes it emerges from the idea that modesty is the faculty that allows human beings to discover that they possess the freedom to restrain themselves (Capograssi 1959, 400).

In other words, modesty manifests itself as a sentiment of boundaries – the foundational feeling of the original juridical relationship, and therefore the basis of the social bond (Savona 2005, 47–48).

This is also the direction suggested by Vico's interpreter Limone:

> Modesty indicates boundaries that are not open to transgression. [...] Once these are crossed, the individual, the social group, the human world reacts – or, alternatively, dissolves.
>
> Modesty, in safeguarding boundaries, alludes to the bond. Like the law, which recalls the bond. Like the law, which secures the bond. (Limone 2004, 66)

---

9 Vico's thought has recently returned to the focus of legal-philosophical analysis (Zanetti 2011), particularly in regard to the recovery of the aesthetic-rhetorical method (Heritier 2016). For further discussion of the Vichian notion of *pudore* (modesty), see Limone (2004); Pons (2005); Dalmasso (2012).

As a movement of juridical sense, in the form most relevant to our discussion here, the notion of modesty resurfaces in Plato's recollection of the myth of Prometheus and Epimetheus, through the term *aidos* in association with *dike*.

As D'Agostino (1979, 31) writes: "Among the numerous and structurally diverse myths in which the theme of the origins of law emerges, the one that Plato places in the mouth of Protagoras [...] has particular significance, because it traces law [...] to a precise existential attitude of recognition of the other." He further emphasizes, regarding the meaning of *aidos* in its pairing with *dike*, that "*aidos* is not only a self-limitation of the 'I,' but also a demand that the other limit themselves in relation to the 'I'" (*ibid.*, 36), thus discerning the necessary reciprocity in respecting boundaries at the level of interindividual relations.

Within this distance, necessary for coexistence, the opening and the coming of the sense of the Other take place – where thirdness, the concern of the entire social group, is touched and the juridical is embodied.

On the legal value of this particular notion of *aidos* associated with *dike* – in terms of the assumption of responsibility – Limone writes:

> On closer inspection, at the moment when *dike* and *aidos* are joined, a new dimension emerges: that *aidos* is not merely modesty toward oneself, but modesty toward one's own action. Indeed, the modesty with which one feels a general sense of respect for oneself and for others extends into a feeling that accompanies action – any action (including a just one) – performed in relation to oneself and to others. One feels modesty not only for oneself and for others, but for the action undertaken in that relationship with oneself and with others. In other words, *aidos* is not only a feeling, but also a limit upon action and a sense of responsibility for that action. Here a new profile takes shape: a modesty *of action*, revealing that actions must bear within themselves the sense of limit and responsibility. (Limone 2019, 16)

The hendiadys *aidos–dike* is not, in itself, new, as it is a recurring motif in other sources as well. However, Plato's narrative is particularly interesting in at least two respects. The first concerns the substance of the story, which is more extensive than in other versions of the myth. The second concerns the problem addressed in the dialogue that frames the story – namely, the teachability of political art, to which the qualities of *aidos* and *dike* pertain.

Hippocrates, a young Athenian eager to become a disciple of Protagoras, goes to Socrates so that he might intercede on his behalf with the philosopher. Protagoras is a sophist – he has no specific trade. By his own account, his skill lies in improving those who associate with him day by day, until he makes of them good citizens. It is Socrates who raises the question, doubting that political art can be taught. He essentially objects that every citizen of Athens, whatever their status or profession, is called upon to exercise political art – to deliberate on matters of civic administration or to offer counsel – without having received any formal instruction. Taking up the challenge, Protagoras decides to support his thesis first by recounting a myth – the tale of Prometheus and Epimetheus – and then by reinforcing it with reasoning.

The story is among the best known. The Titan brothers Prometheus and Epimetheus are charged by the gods with distributing among all living beings destined to inhabit the earth the capacities necessary to survive both the natural environment and the aggression of other living creatures. Persuading his brother to let him carry out the task alone, Epimetheus proceeds with the distribution himself, reserving for Prometheus the role of inspection once the work is complete – but fatally forgets to endow the human creature with the attributes needed for survival.

When Prometheus learns of the problem – after all the gifts have already been distributed and with no means of salvation left for mankind – he steals from Hephaestus and Athena their technical wisdom, along with fire, indispensable for putting that knowledge to use, and bestows these upon man.

"Thus man had the wisdom necessary to the support of life, but political wisdom he had not," Protagoras states (*Protagoras* 322a). Lacking political wisdom, human beings cannot bind themselves together for mutual defense against stronger animals, and so – despite possessing the art of making everything they need – they remain exposed to the risk of extinction.

It is not that human beings fail to understand the value of coming together and securing their survival by founding cities; the problem is that, lacking the political art, they remain divided. Each time they attempt coexistence, Protagoras observes, they are overcome by enmity and mutual harm. At this point, Zeus intervenes. Fearing that humanity would perish without society, the father of the gods commands Hermes to bring to mankind *aidos* and *dike*, so that these may serve as the ordering principles of cities and the generative bonds of friendship. He further instructs Hermes to distribute these two qualities to all, without distinction, unlike the other arts – for cities could not arise if only a few men partook of them. This condition is of such importance that Zeus decrees a law whereby anyone who lacks *aidos* and *dike* shall be put to death as a pest of the city.

> Now man, having a share of the divine attributes, was at first the only one of the animals who had any gods, because he alone was of their kindred; and he would raise altars and images of them. He was not long in inventing articulate speech

> and names; and he also constructed houses and clothes and shoes and beds, and drew sustenance from the earth. Thus provided, mankind at first lived dispersed, and there were no cities. But the consequence was that they were destroyed by the wild beasts, for they were utterly weak in comparison of them, and their art was only sufficient to provide them with the means of life, and did not enable them to carry on war against the animals: food they had, but not as yet the art of government, of which the art of war is a part. After a while the desire of self-preservation gathered them into cities; but when they were gathered together, having no art of government, they evil intreated one another, and were again in process of dispersion and destruction. Zeus feared that the entire race would be exterminated, and so he sent Hermes to them, bearing reverence (*aidos*) and justice (*dike*) to be the ordering principles of cities and the bonds of friendship and conciliation. Hermes asked Zeus how he should impart justice and reverence among men: should he distribute them as the arts are distributed; that is to say, to a favoured few only, one skilled individual having enough of medicine or of any other art for many unskilled ones? "Shall this be the manner in which I am to distribute justice (*dike*) and reverence (*aidos*) among men, or shall I give them to all?" "To all," said Zeus; "I should like them all to have a share; for cities cannot exist, if a few only share in the virtues, as in the arts. And further, make a law by my order, that he who has no part in reverence (*aidos*) and justice (*dike*) shall be put to death, for he is a plague of the state." (*Protagoras* 322a–d)[10]

After concluding the story, Protagoras comments on the myth, affirming that Socrates is right to believe that every human being is by nature endowed with the political art, and that all citizens are necessarily involved in the affairs of communal life. This does not mean, however, that such an art requires no cultivation; rather, it must be developed, and each person must discover it within themselves and learn to exercise it. In this sense, it can indeed be taught – a point Protagoras supports with further philosophical reasoning.

The myth of Prometheus and Epimetheus tells, above all, of relationality as the original condition for the survival of every living being. This is evident, as Gilli observes (1988, 116), in Epimetheus's distribution of attributes to the various species, each in relation to the specific qualities assigned to the others:

10 In the translation adopted here, by B. Jowett, the Greek terms *aidos* and *dike* have been inserted in parentheses at the points where they occur in the Greek text, in order to avoid semantic slippage – particularly with regard to the rendering of *aidos* as "reverence."

> There were some to whom he gave strength without swiftness, while he equipped the weaker with swiftness; some he armed, and others he left unarmed; and devised for the latter some other means of preservation, making some large, and having their size as a protection, and others small, whose nature was to fly in the air or burrow in the ground; this was to be their way of escape.
>
> Thus did he compensate them with the view of preventing any race from becoming extinct. (*Protagoras* 320e–321a)

But that is not all. To this structural arrangement of functional interdependence among the various species, the story adds a distribution of qualities enabling living beings to endure environmental hardship:

> And when he had provided against their destruction by one another, he contrived also a means of protecting them against the seasons of heaven; clothing them with close hair and thick skins sufficient to defend them against the winter cold and able to resist the summer heat, so that they might have a natural bed of their own when they wanted to rest; also he furnished them with hoofs and hair and hard and callous skins under their feet. Then he gave them varieties of food-herb of the soil to some, to others fruits of trees, and to others roots, and to some again he gave other animals as food. And some he made to have few young ones, while those who were their prey were very prolific; and in this manner the race was preserved. (*Protagoras* 321a–b)

The original condition of living beings is therefore relational and marked by diversity (Gilli 1988, 143) – both in the reciprocal relationships among the various animal species and in their relationship with the natural environment.

The only creature excluded from this distributive network is the human being, who, by fate, deprived of any natural quality for survival, is endowed by Prometheus with technical knowledge and, through this sharing of art with Hephaestus and Athena, becomes the only animal both intelligent and devout toward the gods.

This circumstance, together with the system of distribution, clearly alters the very quality of the relationship that arises between mankind and the other living species, as well as its broader connection with the environment, for humanity learns to govern its being-in-the-world unidirectionally – overcoming its deficiencies and confronting adversaries and adversity through technique.

The fact that Protagoras emphasizes the lack of functional interdependence – and hence reciprocity – between the human species and the others may foreshadow mankind's tendency to abstract itself from its belonging to nature. Yet it is more plausible that the sophist, by highlighting the existence in the human world of a division of labor through the redistribution of technical and professional skills, intended to show how, even within the human sphere, the fact of diversity persists. Consequently, relationality for human beings appears as an equally original condition, though one more closely tied to the political community, to which humans necessarily belong – with the difference that, among human beings, this relationality is not automatic but must be sustained: it requires friendship.

Here, the reasons for Zeus's intervention become clear. Since humans risk their own survival through their incapacity to live as citizens, Zeus decrees the endowment of the political art, whose necessary qualities are *aidos* and *dike* – which, unlike professional skills, must be given to everyone equally. Moreover, it is not permissible, Zeus declares, for anyone to lack them within themselves, on pain of death.

The reversal of the distributive logic that underlies the undifferentiated bestowal of political qualities has been interpreted as clear evidence of the idea that the human city can exist only among equal citizens (Gilli 1988, 165 ff.). In this respect, the association of *aidos* and *dike* makes it possible to balance the demands of alterity within the shared horizon of the city, clarifying that if *aidos* is the pre-condition for respect toward oneself and toward others, *dike* extends this feeling of limit to every citizen, safeguarding relations among citizens in their mutual otherness. It is as if to say that, within the distance imposed by modesty, all must be equally respectful of one another, drawing upon a sentiment that enables each person to preserve both themselves and the other within the relationship.

Yet the bond between *aidos* and *dike* does not end there. In this primordial dimension, *dike* connects with *aidos* above all through its substantive reference to the duty of care for the relationship incumbent upon every citizen – a duty that, as we shall soon see, finds explicit expression in the notion of *adikia*, thus linking *dike* once again to the juridical, within the space of thirdness opened by alterity, whose respect is vital for the survival of human relations and of the city.

In short, the hendiadys *aidos–dike* reflects the idea that one becomes a true citizen – that is, capable of sustaining political coexistence – only by assuming responsibility for alterity and sociality. And this can happen only if one is endowed with modesty and justice, in other words, animated by juridical sentiment.

For a human being to become *politikos*, however, the genetic element alone does not suffice. The second part of the dialogue addresses the question of whether political art can be taught, precisely so that Protagoras may affirm that *dike* and *aidos* are virtues that the good citizen must cultivate through study and practice, within a *paideia* aimed at deepening awareness: one must know that one has within oneself *aidos* and *dike*, Protagoras says. Only by cultivating this sensibility, we might add, can one question sense – thus opening oneself to the coming of the juridical.

Before law – this is the echo that rises from the Platonic dialogue – there lies juridical sentiment, born of the capacity to safeguard thirdness within the modest distance of a mutually respectful relation. In this sense, as Vogliotti notes (2007, 315), more than the force of established rules, what matters is the strength of the person who knows how to cultivate their own humanity: "The fate of law does not depend solely on its rules or on the possession of a refined *techne*, but also, and above all, on the *ethos* of its actors and, in particular, on the internalization […] of the sense of limit." D'Agostino echoes this view (1979, 45): "Law, for human beings, is something to be recognized and achieved; it is not a given, but a task."

Plato deliberately refrains from re-counting how, even in his time, the sentiment of modesty had already been lost through the separation of *aidos* and *dike*.

As Hesiod foresaw:

> There will be no favor for the man who keeps his oath or for the just or for the good; but rather men will praise the evil-doer and his violent dealing. Strength will be right (*dike*), and reverence (*aidos*) will cease to be; and the wicked will hurt the worthy man, speaking false words against him, and will swear an oath upon them. (*Works and Days* 190–93)

Yet this does not refer only to the danger of justice being reduced to a mere instrument of power. Jaeger (1944) perceives in this development the advance of democracy and its tendency toward rationalization, privileging the formalized order of *dike* over that of *aidos* – the heroic and aristocratic sentiment *par excellence*, whose time, celebrated for centuries in Homeric poetry, had come to an end.

Aidos has given way to *dike*, but Plato restores it to the field so that its value may not be lost – for there is no justice without a sense of boundaries, without the respect that arises from feeling modesty. And he seems to tell us that, since there are no longer men capable of blushing, the time has come to teach the worth and virtue of doing so.

3.3 *Adikia*

"Without *dike*" is the most intuitive translation of *adikia*, yet it may also prove the most revealing once the complex meaning of the term is unearthed and the semantic scope of *dike* enriched by new elements.

In its usual sense of "injustice," with all its terminological derivatives, *adikia* ordinarily refers to violent, criminal, or harmful behavior – acts of appropriation of what belongs to others – and, in this sense, there is little to add to the exhaustive analysis of the sources offered by Gernet (1917, 35–95). However, by following a less-traveled path, one can uncover in *adikia* a far more original and primordial meaning – one that once again reveals the significance of juridical sentiment in relation to the Other.

A first trace of the term is preserved in the famous fragment of Anaximander (DK 12 B1). The translation most widely used in Anglophone literature is that proposed by Guthrie (1962):

> Whence things have their origin, there too their passing away occurs, according to necessity; for they pay penalty and render justice to one another for their injustice, according to the ordinance of time. (Anaximander, DK 12 B1)

The interpretation of this fragment is among the most controversial issues in classical studies. Neither the complexity of the text nor the doubts concerning the partial or total authenticity of the saying attributed to Anaximander – transmitted by Simplicius (who himself derived it from Theophrastus) – make the task any easier; these difficulties are further compounded by the temporal and cultural distance separating Anaximander from his earliest transmitter.

The version adopted by Colli (2006), within the limits of the present discussion, introduces the line of inquiry that concerns us here. Rendered in English, it reads:

> The things from which the things that are have their coming-to-be are, moreover, those toward which their ruin also develops, according to what must be; for the things that are suffer, from one another, punishment and vengeance for their injustice (*didonai … diken kai tisin allelois tes adikias*), according to the decree of Time. (Colli 2006, 155)

The fragment's central theme is the relationship between origin (the things out of which) and the coming-to-be of all entities (the things that are). According to what must be, from the undifferentiated whole of the origin, each being arises only to decline again, returning to its source. This law of necessity manifests itself in the temporal realm as an opposition among all beings, who punish one another (*diken kai tisin allelois*) for their injustice (*adikia*).

All are guilty, Anaximander seems to affirm, by virtue of their very being – guilty simply because they *are*, because they exist as distinct and individuated entities, separated in their singularity from the origin.

Heidegger notes, in the long essay he devotes to this fragment in *Off the Beaten Track*, that Anaximander employs juridical language – terms commonly used in the daily life of the *polis* – but with a much broader meaning: "far-reaching, rich, and containing much that has been thought out" (Heidegger 2002, 250). He writes:

> [...] the saying says nothing of payment, penalty, or damages. Nor does it say that something is punishable or must be avenged (according to the opinion of those who equate vengeance with justice). (Heidegger 2002, 268)

For the German philosopher, *dike*, *adikia*, and *tisis* describe the movement of becoming in Being: the being-present, that which stays awhile and appears in forms of perpetual transformation – that is, in "the things that are," the individuated beings of which Anaximander speaks – caught between the necessary law of becoming and the will to persistence, exposed to the acceptance of a destiny of indeterminacy and to the transience of dwelling. In this dynamic, "*Dike*[...] is the ordering, jointure-giving order," whereas "*Adikia*, dis-jointure, is Dis-order" (Heidegger 2002, 269).

Heidegger discerns within this flux two tensions: that of ordering and jointure-giving order, marked by *dike*, which embraces "what must be," and that of disjointure and disorder, which in *adikia* asserts the claim to remain present. Yet there is no conflict: between the two tensions, the higher law of becoming prevails, for in each case what presences lets order belong.

In Heidegger's reading of Anaximander, there is none of the "metaphysical pessimism" that Colli (2006, 30) identifies – namely, that "birth is guilt and injustice, death expiation, and vengeance." Heidegger instead perceives the movement of becoming in the rhythmic individuation of things that are, in their being, both life and death. Every being stretches itself within *adikia* because it seeks to continue to be – it resists death – yet it is at the same time informed by the tension toward ordering, by *dike*, which both precedes and surpasses *adikia*, since it accepts the transience of dwelling.

Each thing that stays awhile therefore does not rise up against the others. The thing that is – being a transitory form of staying awhile – does not stubbornly persist in its presentness (which is also its singularity), thereby becoming inconsiderate of the other. On the contrary, "they, things which stay awhile, let one thing belong to another: consideration toward each other" (Heidegger 2002, 271).

In this sense, Heidegger's interpretation of the term *tisis* is revealing, since, according to the philosopher, it allows one to discern what better captures the essential meaning of paying heed and esteeming, and, more specifically, the idea of *reck*:

> Insofar as things which stay awhile are not entirely abandoned to the boundless fixation on aggrandizing themselves into sheerly persisting continuants – a craving which leads them to seek to expel one another from what is presently present – they let order belong – *didonai diken.*
>
> Insofar as things which stay awhile give order, they thereby allow, in their relationship to each other, reck to belong, in every case each allowing it to belong to the other – *didonai … kai tisin allelois.* (Heidegger 2002, 272)

Within the horizon of a destiny shared by all beings, the fragment thus seems to reveal, in Heidegger's view, that the resolution of disorder is achieved precisely through *reck* – through the mutual care that one being extends toward another. This also means that *adikia* is associated not only with disjointure and disorder – the obstinate persistence of being in its own singularity – but also with a form of careless or inconsiderate care.

Let us turn to a second indication. Gilli (1988, 328) identifies it in relation to the idea of "doing injustice," finding it – among other sources[11] – in several verses of Sappho from the fragment known as *Deathless Aphrodite*, where *adikia* appears in its verbal form, *adikein*:

> […] Whom should I persuade (now again)
> to lead you back into her love?
> Who, O Sappho, is wronging you (*adikeei*)?
> For if she flees, soon she will pursue.
> If she refuses gifts, rather will she give them.
> If she does not love, soon she will love
> even unwilling. (*Deathless Aphrodite*, 18–24)

Here, too, the notion of *adikia* cannot be reduced to the narrow sense of justice rendered in response to an offense. The "injustice" that Sappho suffers lies

11 Gilli provides an analysis of numerous passages in which the term *adikia* is used to indicate resistance to various forms of relationship (Gilli 1988, 336–344).

in not being loved in return: "Who, Sappho, is wronging you" – literally, "Who is doing you injustice, Sappho?" – that is, who fails to reciprocate your love?

Nor is this the only fossil of *adikia* in the context of love; there are several, enough to suggest that the injustice of "doing injustice" lies in the absence of reciprocity – in the failure to return the affection of one who, in that affection, has made themselves vulnerable. To do injustice can therefore mean, in other words, to refuse to enter into a relationship desired by another. Thus, rather than referring to directly harmful conduct, it concerns the refusal to enter into relation: "The declaration of 'injustice' always comes from the one who, explicitly inclined toward a relationship, finds themselves rejected by the desired counterpart" (Gilli 1988, 328–331).

Resistance to forming bonds is also found in various other forms of social relations within ancient Greek culture, as in the case just examined of the master–disciple relationship depicted in Plato's *Protagoras*, where Hippocrates suffers the *adikia* of not being accepted by Protagoras as a pupil.

What matters most here is the recognition that within the notion of *adikia* – whether amorous or otherwise affectively marked – lies the refusal to enter into relation with the Other and the denunciation of that refusal. This meaning is so attuned to the sense of *adikia* that one can imagine that this feeling of injustice may stem from the absence of the *reck* invoked by Anaximander – an absence ascribable, as Heidegger suggests, to the being that obstinately persists in its own individuation, resisting both other beings and the originary Other.

Certainly, in Sappho's *Deathless Aphrodite*, *adikia* pertains solely to the human world; yet the resonance between this "injustice" and the meaning that reverberates from Anaximander's fragment is striking. It makes plausible the interpretation of such refusal to respond to another's call for relation as a deliberate withdrawal from a duty of *reck* – a duty incumbent upon human beings as creatures generated from a single origin.

If this is one possible meaning of injustice, it follows that *dike*, although opposed to it, may nonetheless draw upon the same primordial dimension, with the result of disclosing a further element of its complex semantics – one that opens toward an understanding of justice closer to relationality and the duty of care than to equality.

In this sense, there is already an opening – again using Heidegger's expression – to a juridical sense that is "far-reaching," one that acknowledges the original kinship between law and sentiment.

Yet it is worth pursuing a further indication: *adikia* as the refusal to heed a plea for help.

> O Lord Apollo, you know how to do no wrong (*to me adikein*);
> and, since you know this, learn not to be neglectful also.
> For your power to do good is assured. (*Eumenides* 85–87)

It is Orestes who invokes the god. In the play that most fully consecrates justice to the tragic dimension, *Eumenides*, Aeschylus employs *adikia* to identify yet another mode of justice – namely, the duty to respond to the supplicant. This is not Athena's mediation, nor the formal justice that will later emerge with the institution of the Areopagus, but rather the duty to allow oneself to be drawn into a relationship of assistance – to accompany the supplicant in his plight, and to protect the validity of his cause.

Apollo, indeed, does not turn away. To the Erinyes, who demand that the matricide be surrendered to them, he replies:

> And I will aid my suppliant and rescue him! For the wrath of the one who seeks purification is terrible among mortals and gods, if I intentionally abandon him. (*Eumenides* 232–234)

Before juridical mediation or the tribunal, thanks to the notion of *adikia*, *dike* thus signifies – within the framework of the *reck* that human beings owe one another – the duty to respond to a plea for help.

It is this same justice that leads Arete to Odysseus, as she responds to the plea for help from the wretched stranger who has clasped her knees. In this passage of the *Odyssey* – one of the most symbolically charged in the entire history of Western narrative – hospitality is assumed as a duty: the duty to enter into the hospitable relation, whatever may follow (Mittica 2006, 2007). More than that, it is the capacity to take upon oneself another's suffering – not through identification, but through attention, respect, and *reck*. Arete is not empathetic; as the emblem of virtue, as we have seen above, the queen of the Phaeacians allows her duty to respond and to bind herself – which is a form of obligation – to take its course.

The sentiment that must accompany openness to the Other is, in this case too, powerfully and juridically defined, and as such remains inscribed in the iconography of justice through the centuries. The uncovered knee is its visible sign (Sbriccoli 2009, 204) – a reminder, like an invisible thread, that the justice of the sword is also composed of this more original *dike*.

The theme is dear to Simone Weil:

> For Weil, justice is not realized through a rule; it is realized instead in the individual gesture of one who perceives another's need and acts accordingly.

> [...]
> This means that justice is realized only where there is someone capable of seeing affliction and hearing the desperate cry of one in need.
> [...]
> Justice requires vision, and vision can be exercised only through the practice of attention. The just person is one who constantly seeks the face of the one who needs help; the just person is one who lowers themselves; the just person is one who refrains from using the force they could use.
>
> "Attention," therefore, but also "listening" and "knowing" things: listening in silence to what is often nothing but a silent cry (for the afflicted have no voice); knowledge-as-intuition that allows one to see beyond what appears on the surface. (Greco 2009, 113–115)

Tommaso Greco's great merit lies in tracing within Weil's thought the contours of this form of justice, revealing its profound affinity with the idea of sensitive thought – a thinking stretched toward the coming of sense from attentiveness, understood as listening and *reck* of alterity, or as a form of thirdness preserved within the mystery of being-in-common, for which each person bears responsibility before every other human being and every other living being. Thus, law must be discerned as sense composed in silence, arising from the emergence of feeling, sentiment, and reasoning that the Other awakens.

If this is justice, then the just person is the one who chooses to set limits for themselves.

4 The Art of the Jurist

Romano writes:

> Between the art of the jurist and the know-how of the technician of norms no mediation is possible; art takes its model from the bond between word and silence, know-how from number. (Romano 2006, 175)

If we understand juridicality as a formative process through which juridical forms are instituted and animated by juridical sentiment, then the jurist-artist is the one who experiences this feeling – who thinks with the thinking of the body, who is capable of listening and giving voice to this sensibility. Thirdness is the horizon of their inquiry; *reck* of being-in-common is their aim.

Like Greek *poiesis*, the art of the jurist is a *techne* that unites scientific–technical skill and poetic *virtus* within a single sensibility. As has been repeatedly observed, the capable jurist must learn the art of sensitive thought, for only through such attentiveness can juridical sense arise – the only kind that opens, within the horizon of thirdness, a sustained openness toward other living beings. It is the art of one who knows how to touch and be touched, who does not turn away from suffering, who cultivates passion and feeling.

By experiencing their own exposure to the Other and dwelling within the openness of limit, the jurist learns the mystery that envelops the things that are; they become familiar with uncertainty, precariousness, and need. In them, juridical sentiment emerges as *reck* of the Other, through the necessity of opposing the measure for being-in-common to the excess of singularity's self-assertion. Thus, they direct their thinking – the thought that weighs – toward the search for juridical form, moving beyond finite meaning stiffened by the formalism and technicalities of juridical bureaucratization, so that a new measure may take shape.

The art of the jurist is the art of limit – if we understand limit, following Cananzi (2016, 165), not as the boundary beyond which one cannot go, but as the very condition of human and meaningful progression. It is also the art of forging the forms in which law takes shape, of becoming a threshold oneself, allowing the juridical form to give expression to the movement from which measure arises. The art of the jurist conceives the norm as *rhythmos*. It consists in the capacity to serve as the conduit through which measure – like a work of art – happens, taking form without closing the flow of sense.

Thus, the new juridical form presents itself as mobile and flexible, open to formative potential. Ultimately, it falls to the jurist, as a bearer of this art, to undertake the demanding task of questioning sense without withdrawing from the flux of forms, and to transform both norms and himself, in the awareness that he never wholly possesses himself (Romano 2006, 313).

But how does one learn this art? How does one learn to open oneself to the coming of the sense of justice and law – stretching from finite forms toward new ones, summoning all the resources of sensibility, both affective and rational? How does one learn, as Rovatti (2007) would say, to inhabit distance in the exercise of speech, reclaiming the capacity to listen to silence?

For the silencing of oneself is not only the condition for listening to the other being who stands before us; it is, above all, the way to deviate from what is already defined, to allow the undefined to touch us, and thus to become able to listen to the Other who insinuates itself into the thirdness of being-in-common.

For the jurist, silence is the condition of sense for words and the responsible preparation for speech itself. More than that, norms possess juridical meaning only within a language that gives form to a partial knowledge, one always ready to reshape itself.

If, in instituting and interpreting norms, the form of the statement is the outcome of what the jurist says as they move from silence – that is, from what remains unsaid – then to take account of the dimension of the unspoken and the unsayable is to weaken the tyranny of the spoken word: to undermine the presumption that law can be made into a total form of knowledge, one capable of engendering fundamentalisms and exclusions (Romano 2006, 146–147).[12]

And once again, then – how does one learn the art? This question inevitably opens the broader chapter of juridical education, to which belongs the extensive debate concerning the profound crisis that is progressively affecting the humanistic dimension of legal education. Here, however, we shall limit ourselves to highlighting the proposal that emerges from the methodology of Law and Humanities.

The history of this movement has already been widely discussed.[13] In light of the various interpretations of the heuristic potential of this pairing, it is enough here to clarify a few essential points.

---

12 The theme of silence has already been addressed in connection with law from multiple perspectives. For the Italian debate, see the collective volume edited by Casucci (2013). Within the international debate, see, for example, Constable (2005).

13 Although constantly evolving, the framework re-constructed by Sarat, Anderson, and Frank (2010) remains largely accurate. These scholars remind us that little progress has been made beyond the original idea underlying the movement, which Guido Calabresi eloquently summarized in his introductory letter for the first issue of the *Yale Journal of Law & Humanities* in 1989: "Law feeds and is fed by the world around it. Fortunately, that world is at least as aptly described and understood by the humanities as by the social and natural sciences. Hence, and also fortunately, it is impossible fully to understand law without a deep and sympathetic knowledge of the liberal arts. But that knowledge cannot be just background; it must be a fundamental part of legal scholarship. Similarly, many a problem in the humanities (and in the sciences) would be better understood if scholars in these fields knew what legal scholars, and law itself, had said to the issue."

Thanks to numerous developments, it now seems that the time has also come for the theoretical scope of Law and Humanities to be broadened in accordance with the advances of Law and Aesthetics, so as to re-establish the connection between law and ethics on deeper foundations, in keeping with an integrated vision of the human being as both existing and exposed. Important anticipations in this direction are offered by Douzinas and Nead (1999); see also Robilant (2001), Faralli (2022). For the Italian experience of Law and Humanities, see the privileged observatory of the Italian Society for Law and Literature (ISLL).

First, what should we understand by the humanities in relation to law?

Under the umbrella of the humanities, we include every work-made-with-art, whatever its expressive form and whatever artistic or cultural genre it may belong to – understanding by this any work capable of initiating a process of opening to sense, that is, of opening the transformative space of experience. Even the most canonical work of art must be approached not through the canons of art history – or, still worse, of the art market – but through the tension awakened by the wonder it stirs in those who encounter it (Mittica 2021).

On the juridical side, law is also understood in an extended sense as encompassing the entire juridical field through which juridical sense–sentiment flows, comprising actors, interpreters, and juridical forms.

By virtue of the relationship established in the pairing law and the humanities, these two terms therefore express the possibility of bringing the juridical field into dialogue with art *tout court* – engaging in a sustained critique of juridical formalism from multiple perspectives, but above all opening new pathways of understanding so that the jurist may cultivate the art of law.

It is also worth clarifying that the work capable of shaping a jurist's formation need not necessarily provide a representation of law or justice as such. Although this has been the prevailing tendency in much of the research within Law and Humanities field, the work in question need not depict justice or denounce injustice, nor must it serve as a "mirror of law." What matters is the work that resonates with the jurist, that unsettles and moves them – allowing for deviation: for the apprehension of a possible subversion of established canons, for an opening toward the unthought, for a stretching of imagination and perception.

In this sense, the perspective offered by Law and Aesthetics goes beyond the more traditional approaches of Law in/Law as (Literature, Cinema, etc.), situating itself within the broader horizon of formativity (Pareyson 1954) and showing that the forms realized through art constitute the most vital human forge of meaning, juridical meaning included, precisely because they are imbued with an ethical quality.

A work of art is a form that appears and shakes us. Opening like a threshold, it creates a space in which one can stretch toward understanding the Other. To engage with a work is to engage with an outside dimension; it allows one to experience tangibly the touch of the Other – that which makes us aware of the finitude and irreducibility of alterity. It helps one grow familiar with sensitive thought, which opens itself, listens, awaits the Other, and, in weighing, gives one to think.

By entering into relation with a work, the jurist also enters into work upon themselves, learning to travel paths – including inner ones – along which cognitive resources are expanded through contact with a sense articulated not only conceptually but also materially, sensorially, and emotionally. This disposition prepares one for the coming of juridical sense-sentiment, for *reck* of the Other, and for the care of being-in-common.

Our proposal is simple – though only in its formulation. Since we hold that to learn, or to re-learn, the art of law requires refining both the aesthetic and ethical sensibility of those called to interrogate sense, the way forward is to lead the jurist toward an authentic encounter with the work-made-with-art, employing the Law and Humanities approach chiefly for this purpose.

The hope is that the jurist may learn the art of listening and giving voice to the juridical sense-sentiment as it arises, so as to understand and give form to the most just measure.

CHAPTER 3

Practices in Law and Humanities

1 Engaging with the Work

To open oneself at the threshold – within the liminal space of alterity – one must loosen the grip of passion for rationality and individualism, yielding instead to the reasonableness of feeling.

The thinking that gives-to-think is essential for the jurist to prepare for the coming of juridical sense-sentiment, in attentiveness to the Other and in care for being-in-common. An understanding capable of embracing uncertainty is born of experience, and it is a matter of the body – of the body's consistency and its presence to its own sensations (Jedlowski 2008, 168).

Yet our thinking can reveal its sensibility and comprehend only if we learn to listen, just as the form we express can find its rhythm only when we are able to welcome the transformation that comes from our relation to an outside.

This is a technique that requires the refinement of aesthetic and ethical sensibility and can only be grounded in experience. Indeed, there is no other way to interrogate sense than by placing oneself in the condition for it to emerge – by opening oneself to experience.

For the jurist, this involves learning the art of listening and speaking – that is, of receiving the feeling in which measure takes root, grasping its pathic dimension, and translating it into norm, while integrating this process with their technical and formal competence.

Although aware that every judgment – the decision of a judge or any other evaluative act that gives rise to a norm – is, as Cananzi (2017a, 15) puts it, only an unfinished, powerless, and insufficient moment in the life of law, the jurist may refine an understanding that necessarily precedes action, including its affective component. In doing so, the jurist may give form to a more just norm – one closer to, and recognizable by, those who await acknowledgment in their expectations of law, thereby safeguarding the social bond.

The encounter with the work may be what sets this process in motion. This is why Law and Humanities become such a fruitful methodology: by combining the two domains of making-with-art and the juridical, it provides the jurist with the appropriate tools and sensibilities to approach an experience that is at once aesthetic and ethical – one that begins in the authentic encounter with the work-made-with-art. Indeed, by entering into relation with the work, the jurist enters into work upon themselves, learning to walk paths –

HTTPS://DOI.ORG/10.1163/9789004757714-005

also within themselves – along which cognitive and expressive resources expand, drawing synesthetically upon sensibility itself.

But how can this experience be activated in practice? Where does one begin?

The flow of experience is always prompted by something we perceive as an external event. In this sense, the work *happens*: it enters our perception as an unexpected irruption, a shock that displaces us and carries us elsewhere.

Whatever its form or circumstance, the encounter with the work compels us, first of all, to reexamine our relationship with things and with our own body.

On the one hand, the surprise that comes from without – provoked by art and, at once, by the alterity of the artist who has fashioned the object – creates a distance that prevents appropriation or identification. As we have seen, the stirring arises from the occurrence of something that moves us and presents itself in a form – precisely, in the work. There are multiple, sometimes innumerable, ways to define that form by resorting to patterns of meaning we have already codified, yet none can fully express the sense into which we have come – or are coming – through its happening. Of that something, or likewise of that someone, what shakes us is the indefinable: the touch of the Other, which opens the distance where what eludes us may dwell.

On the other hand, the capacity for wonder, together with our emotional and sensory involvement, gives consistency to the body, awakening the awareness that we exist within the limits of our corporeality, and that our thinking – inasmuch as it becomes aware of its own sensibility – is therefore finite. Precisely because we know ourselves to be limited – because we allow the touch of the Other to make us present – the thinking of the body can become openness and listening within the horizon of ethics: ethics understood, as before, as an ethics of finitude (Natoli 2010a).

In brief, the encounter with the work is the experience that enables the one who interrogates sense to gain clarity about themselves, to open as an exposed being, and to reach toward alterity.

The first suggestion, then, is to let oneself be taken by the work – to allow the work to find us in our intimacy, to let it happen, so that we ourselves may come to happen.

The second suggestion is to place one's trust in artistic works. Those who affirm the ethical quality of the work of art are right (Andreotti 2018). Although every form made with art has the potential to lead us to the threshold of sense, it is true that artistic works fulfill this task most fully, for they are already the outcome of an artist's own search for sense – an artifex endowed with heightened or more seasoned sensibility, supported by specific technical and expressive skills. This results in the creation of forms of particular expressive power: original, capable of overturning established canons and thus revealing the unthought, arousing wonder, and prompting transformation.

Illuminating in this regard are the lectures delivered by Kiefer at the Collège de France between 2010 and 2011 on artistic practice (Kiefer 2011). According to Andreotti (2018), when works are made with art, the touch of the Other remains imprinted in them: it is what the artist has been able to feel and to express in a form that, for the one who encounters it, opens a path toward the coming of sense.

For this experience to bear fruit, however, care must be taken in how one approaches it. Even when attempting to interpret the work through the lenses of art history or criticism – more or less improvised – there is a risk of attributing to the work the meaning we would like it to have, without truly entering into relation with it. Moreover, the work does not answer any question about life, nor does it reveal any secret that could be uncovered through analytical methods. It is therefore pointless to seek meaning in this way.

Certainly, the skills required to decode the canons employed in the formal creation of the work or to contextualize the historical and cultural conditions in which it found expression – as well as biographical knowledge of its author – can be helpful, but only as a means of approaching a language not always familiar to us. That said, our relationship with the work must remain entrusted to a sensitive approximation. This is what ensures the authenticity of the event, of which the work – the thing that stands before us – becomes both the proof and the testimony, even of that which we cannot put into words but which, as it happens, we feel.

A third suggestion is to give oneself time.

The work demands attention, silence, and listening – in a word, time. It unfolds in waiting, like the coming of sense itself. It calls for a kind of regard that matures, quite literally, through looking again and again, each time a little more deeply. To remain with the work is an excellent exercise in learning how to stand before the Other: to linger, through this repeated act of looking, in a constant play of encounter and withdrawal that becomes a training ground for the feeling of modesty, better preparing one to seek measure.

On the one hand, the relationship with the work reveals the limit of one's gaze: the detail not yet seen calls us back once more to the finitude of our seeing. On the other hand, the work exposes us to the trembling of our being, against which we learn to offer resistance – containing our suffering (*pathos*) without denying it, and, above all, turning it fruitfully toward an attitude of respect for the Other and responsibility for the Other, as a duty of care within the horizon of being-in-common.

In an extended reflection on the temporalities of law, Ost (1999) argues that law functions as a measure in at least four directions, ranging from the norm to time itself: by taking measures, by using law as an instrument of measurement, by defining the just proportion of things, and by tempering situations. From this perspective, rhythm is to time what measure is to law. In its ongoing work of continual adjustment, juridical measure is rhythm, Ost concludes – and it touches on the most original notion of form, that of *rhythmos*, as well as on temperance in its primordial bond with prudence.

Slowness and duration sit uneasily within a conception of time surrendered to the ever-increasing speed of the world and resigned to the agendas of our daily lives (Han 2017a). Relating to the work, by contrast, moves against this current. To dwell with the work requires the time needed for the movement of sense to unfold. It is the time of *aion* – stretched toward infinity – yet translated into the present of the one who happens with the work; a time of waiting and attention that does not deny but momentarily displaces *khronos*, allowing one to linger on the threshold, to take one's time. For the jurist, it is the time of work-made-with-art – the time that lets *kairos*, the opportune moment, occur.

Thus, against the tyranny of the technostructure's frenzied pace, the one who interrogates sense must slow down – must take the time that is needed. The time of law is a durational present: the time of risk inherent in relation to the Other, of comprehension, openness, and striving toward possibility; the time attuned to respect and responsibility for the Other amid the ceaseless reconfiguration of our shared world. For this reason, above all, the time of law is the time of trust.

> So, we have entered there where we will never enter, into this scene painted on a canvas. All at once, there we are. We can't exactly say that we have penetrated there, but neither can we say that we are outside. We are there in a manner older and simpler than by any movement, displacement, or penetration. We are there without leaving the threshold, on the threshold, neither inside nor outside – and perhaps we are, ourselves, the threshold, just as our eye conforms to the plane of the canvas and weaves itself into its fabric.
> [...]
> Let us not, however, seek to go behind the canvas; rather than trying to see behind the visible, let us not seek anything other than the brief immobilization of the oil. We have entered, already; we are exposed to seeing; that is all we are asked, that is all we are permitted, and that is all we are promised. By a device which is far from being unique in painting, but which here finds one of its chosen places, the canvas signals to us, makes us this sign: Enter and look. Come and see. Exhaust your looks until your eyes close, until your hands are raised over them,

> until your faces fall upon your knees. See the invisible. This is the ordinary command or demand of painting: very simple, very humble, even derisory. See the invisible, not beyond the visible, nor inside, nor outside, but right at it, on the threshold, like its very oil, its weave, and its pigment. (Nancy 1996, 57, 59)

The canvas to which Nancy refers is *The Death of the Virgin* by Caravaggio. In just a few lines, the French philosopher distills the very experience of encountering a work of art.

The work happens independently of both the artist who created it and those who have enjoyed or interpreted it. In this sense, it is autonomous, though it exists in potential – living authentically only through those who enter into resonance with it. Its happening is the happening of a subject suddenly exposed, stretched upon a threshold – becoming a threshold. "Just as our eye conforms to the plane of the canvas and weaves itself into its fabric," writes Nancy, for it is sensitive thought that reflects upon this new condition. The space is that of the threshold, where sensibility stretches and awaits the coming of sense. One must stay with the work, *in opera*, taking time until the gaze is exhausted, "until your eyes close, until your hands are raised over them, until your face falls upon your knees."

Only then will the invisible emerge – not elsewhere, beyond the threshold, in some possible canon, not in something other than what it is, but as the invisible itself: that which we cannot see yet know to be there, in the color, in the trace of the oil, in the movement of the gesture reflected in the brushstroke. The invisible is what we understand without attempting to explain it – what we encounter and with which we come to terms.

Givone (2003) confirms that art is necessary so as not to lose sense, especially in what remains enigmatic within form. "What interests me is the possibility that the object might be something else," says Anish Kapoor (2015). Without art, we would lose the ability to express and communicate all that knowledge cannot say. For the jurist, this would mean closing the form – denying the law itself and, with it, the reasons and hopes of being-in-common.

2 Mary and Gabriel

We stand before *The Annunciation* by Fra Angelico, in the north corridor of the convent of San Marco in Florence. From the outset, we find ourselves drawn to a story we know well, deeply rooted in our tradition – that of Mary.

A guidebook explains that the scene is rendered in a sober style and simple symbolism, intended for meditation rather than ornamentation:

> The episode is set in a loggia, seen in perspective and completely whitewashed. There is no furniture except for a simple stool; the Virgin is a young girl dressed in a modest robe (recalling the Dominican habit), and the Archangel Gabriel displays two beautiful wings with peacock feathers painted in the colors of the rainbow. The artist chose to retain the ancient angelic iconography, dating back to the late thirteenth century, which features elements of the peacock – a symbol of divine wisdom – and of the rainbow – a symbol of God's presence among mankind. With their multicolored wings, angels bear witness to the renewed covenant between God and humanity. Gabriel has just pronounced the announcement and waits, trembling, for her reply. Mary, humble and obedient, folds her hands over her chest and prepares to speak her *fiat*. In the background, a fence encloses an *hortus conclusus*, symbolizing a paradise closed to mankind after original sin, but which, through the Virgin's act of obedience (the new Eve) and Christ's sacrifice (the new Adam), will reopen its gates. (Nifosì 2020)

We look again at the fresco, recognizing the details suggested by the art historian's reading: the white of the portico, the simplicity of the furnishings and garments, the color of the angel's wings, the *hortus conclusus*. With closer attention, we also perceive the perfect geometry of the spatial composition and the chromatic harmony achieved by the painter – and we might be ready to move on with our visit. Yet we pause. A doubt arises. Why do we like it? What makes this work so compelling, so capable of responding to our desire for art and of justifying our being here?

As Jauss (1982) writes, in aesthetic pleasure, the imaginative consciousness is released from the constraints of habits and interests, allowing the individual, prisoner of convention, to open to other forms of experience. Perhaps it is the search for this pleasure that moves us?

So we pause and look again, setting aside our interest in Fra Angelico, his symbolism, or fifteenth-century Florence. We begin to notice that the loggia framing the scene of the *Annunciation* not only opens onto an enclosed garden but is itself distinctly bounded by the portico's arch, beyond which the garden appears to extend still further. Through the small grated window painted in the background, at the center of the fresco, we glimpse yet another garden view; and beyond the fence enclosing it, the landscape stretches into infinity among scattered trees. Above all, the entire scene is suffused with a light descending from outside and from above, illuminating the space between Mary and Gabriel.

The play of light brushes the forms and brightens the intimacy of that interval – it holds us there.

Suddenly, it happens: we find ourselves before a representation of boundaries opening one onto another. All boundaries open as thresholds – onto the Other, onto something we feel exists, yet can only hope to imagine.

The whiteness of the loggia, poised between the closed interior and the open portico, reveals a space of discretion that lends itself to hospitality. The light that floods the encounter between the two figures, descending from outside and from above, marks the further threshold between the human and the divine – the one that opens for Mary as she accepts the mystery of the sacred revealed to her by Gabriel. And further away, beyond the fence, lies the adventure of the world.

We pause again. The light seems to fall directly upon the Virgin, and we sense that, leaning toward her own human limit, this young woman opens herself to the Unknown embodied in the angel, to receive her destiny. The narrative is clear and recognizable – the encounter is hers alone. Yet, without realizing it, for an indeterminate time we too have been standing on the threshold of ourselves: attentive and taut within an unexpected opening of meaning, receptive – through the renewed awareness of our own sensitive thought – to the irreducible alterity that the perception of limit reveals to us.

The experience is meaningful. We have learned the value of pausing, of paying attention, of looking again. This exercise of the eye has led us to recognize the boundaries that embody one of the jurist's deepest anxieties, and to reflect on the presence of the Other, perceived as the reflection of our own incompleteness.

Our visit ends.

Some time later, we encounter *The Annunciation of Mary* by Rainer Maria Rilke:

> The angel's entrance (you must realise)
> was not what made her frightened. The surprise
> he gave her by his coming was no more
> than sun – or moon-beam stirring on the floor
> would give another, – she had long since grown
> used to the form that angels wear, descending;
> never imagining this coming-down
> was hard for them. […]
> No, not to see him enter, but to find
> the youthful angel's countenance inclined
> so near to her; that when he looked, and she
> looked up at him, their looks so merged in one
> the world outside grew vacant suddenly,

> and all things being seen, endured and done
> were crowded into them: just she and he;
> eye and its pasture, visions and its view,
> here at this point and at this point alone:-
> see, this arouses fear. Such fear both knew.

On the threshold of the fresco – and of himself – Rilke falls silent. He observes the play of light moving across the loggia and allows himself to be drawn into its rhythm. He closes his eyes to reach toward the invisible, as Nancy would say. And there it is: within the space that opens before him, a young girl appears, unaware of angels, meeting the gaze of another youth. All around is emptiness. In the silence, there is no longer the story of the Madonna and the Archangel Gabriel, nor the time and space in which Rilke stands. Nowhere else but here. In no time but now. Attention, senses, and meaning – all converge in the encounter through which the mystery – sought, reached, and endured by millions of other eyes – moves between them.

Once again, almost unknowingly, we happen. Rilke's poem becomes the new form that allows that story, that fresco, to draw so close that it becomes our own gaze, our own tenderness.

Rilke penetrates sense all the way to the Other and returns to us its most authentic and primordial sentiment: fear – ancestral, instinctive, and true. We feel it; it is our own – a profoundly human fear that rises within us yet never turns into terror. What prevents it is the sense of measure carefully inscribed in every verse: a measure that we can now also perceive in the proportion and composure of the fresco, gently touched by light.

It is a fear that does not paralyze but invites action – with prudence and tenderness. Like Mary and Gabriel, we may let it be wrapped in delicacy and measure. It is a fear that is reciprocal, intimate, and belongs to each of us, yet it does not lead to withdrawal. Rather, it becomes an opening – a movement toward encounter, carried by gentleness, respect, and responsibility for the Other who draws near.

On the threshold of Rilke's words, our understanding stretches further, offering a new shade of insight into the quality of meeting the Other.

Beyond the fence, the great adventure of the world calls.

3 *Casa d'altri*

> – I have a goat that I always take with me. I have a goat. And my life is the same as hers: exactly the same.

I was about to say something. But she gestured for me to wait.

[...]

– A goat's life, and nothing else. Only she ... How long can a goat live?
– A goat? How long does a goat live? Six or seven years, more or less – I said, caught off guard – as long as she's one of ours.
– Exactly. Six or seven, and that's it. Only she finishes much sooner. Not even comparable ... I'll be sixty-three this winter.

She fell silent and turned to look down into the valley, at the village and all the other villages, shrouded in darkness or visible under the moon.

– No. This isn't my home. This is someone else's home. I know that. And for me, it's just like being here as a lodger. (D'Arzo 2002, 99–100)

Casa d'altri (*Someone Else's Home*) is a short story by Silvio D'Arzo, who died of leukemia in 1952 at just 32, a few months before the publication of what is now regarded as his finest work. "A perfect story," wrote Montale in 1954 in the *Corriere della Sera.*

Born in Reggio Emilia, Italy, in 1920 to an unknown father, he was registered at birth as Ezio Comparoni. Silvio D'Arzo was merely the last of several pseudonyms under which he published, concealing his identity even from his publishers. His biographers portray a poor boy who completed a degree in literature thanks to merit-based scholarships – a young man who bore hardship with dignity, yet also with ambition.

The modesty (*aidos*) we imagine to have marked Ezio Comparoni's life pervades this story of an encounter between an old woman and an old priest. Two very different existences, sharing the same weariness and discontent with life, set against the backdrop of a harsh, cold, desolate countryside – someone else's home, indeed, for both of them: for the old woman, who wishes to end her life, and for the priest, who has lost the sense of his calling. Both are, in their own way, wild creatures, observing one another from a distance – wary, solitary, defiant. Yet both seek dialogue, in the unconscious hope of receiving from the other some meaning for themselves, though words themselves are, for both, a source of shame.

The story is a long waiting – for one another – until the old woman finally frees herself from her torment, questioning the parish priest about the legitimacy of suicide, and he remains helpless, ashamed of himself and of all the words in the world.

– And I thought that now God could do me one small favor, because I've never asked Him for anything. I've never bothered Him, not even this much, in nearly sixty-three years. And I've never held anything against Him – not once. Not even when the mule's kick threw me onto that pile of stones, or when the boys, for a joke, hid half my rags and I had to pay them that very day. But at the time, I didn't know it was just a joke. He could do me a favor, that's all.

She stopped again, for now she was truly moved. And I kept looking at her, and waiting, and said nothing.

– That's why I came to you that evening, to ask whether even you – you churchmen – sometimes don't pay too much heed to the rule: and that story about marriage was just a pretext. And all night long I was ashamed of myself for it.
– That, yes. That I realized right away too – barely three minutes later.
– But you were a little angry, though.
– I said three minutes later, Zelinda. And if I didn't see it right off, it's because by now I'm just another old cab horse. But I did understand, I tell you – and I even called you back for that reason.
– Yes, on the church steps, I know. But that was easy to understand. That one you could see in a flash. But what was inside that letter – you can't understand that. Not you, not "the others" either. And you wouldn't say yes to it, not for all the gold in the world.
– Don't say that, Zelinda – I said in another tone, while the cold crept up my back and into my head. And I felt my nose sting, as if someone were tearing out my hair. – You must never, ever say that. And now, go on.
– You'll only answer no – she insisted, much more faintly now, and she was beginning to understand that she too wanted to tell me everything, to free herself of everything – of all of it – and she no longer believed her own words, and really I was a bit like a spoiled child. – I feel it already. I know.

But I stayed silent; I kept silent, and I knew she would now say everything.

– So you want to know what was written there, do you? – she asked me.

I only nodded.

– All right – she said – then I'll tell you. But you turn the other way and don't look me in the face.

And I did just that. I swear I turned to the wall, as when someone undresses. And not for a second did it occur to me that anyone seeing us might laugh. In any case, that would be his affair. (D'Arzo 2002, 100–101)

The story is one of a fall – one among countless possible stories of human fallibility and the shame that permeates it. Yet in *Casa d'altri*, what strikes us most is the woman's self-possession, drawn from her sense of modesty: the dignity that demands and obtains respect, and, by reflection, the strength of a closeness that arises between two human beings who nonetheless remain at a distance.

The old woman and the priest are two strangers who meet and understand one another. Zelinda has no wish to change her mind; she seeks someone who will listen. She does not fear the hell promised to sinners. Her need is to communicate to another human being the injustice of her condition – her non-life. And that is precisely what she finds in the old priest, who, taking upon himself her anguish, allows her decision to stand, respecting the boundaries of a choice that overturns the rule, becoming its custodian.

> For three months I went down to the canal every evening, and every evening I found her there with her rags. Her goat rummaged here and there. I would stop on the bank, always as if by chance, never for more than a minute or two – just long enough for the old woman to decide whether or not to acknowledge me. Then I would go back again to the rectory. Not once in three months did she give me the slightest sign, or even raise her head. She was still there – that was all – and from the bank I could see that she was there, and the rest meant nothing. And we both knew perfectly well that we would never speak to each other again, never even greet each other if we met; but even that meant less than nothing.
> […]
> An absurd old woman; an absurd priest; a whole absurd story worth a penny. (D'Arzo 2002, 123)

4 Differently Human

Finch (2021), directed by Miguel Sapochnik, focuses on three central characters: Finch, a robotics engineer played by Tom Hanks; Goodyear, the dog he cares for; and Jeff, the robot endowed with artificial intelligence that he has built. The plot is stripped to its essentials, as is the screenplay itself.

Set in a not-so-distant future ravaged by solar storms, the world has become increasingly desertified, and the struggle for survival has turned mankind into scavengers – nothing particularly original there.

The film opens on Finch's daily life, spent amid dust and searing, unbreathable air, as he searches for water and food among corpses and remnants in looted supermarkets, which he methodically maps after each visit. Sealed in his protective suit, Finch hums to himself and listens to the radio: it is a day like any other, spent in the company of Dewey, the small robot that helps him scavenge whatever little they manage to find. There is, in this routine, a muted and fragile sense of satisfaction. Its cost, however, is unmistakable. Each day he risks being killed by another human or by a sandstorm, and once back inside the bunker he has turned into a home, his ulcers have worsened yet again. Even in this, there is little that surprises.

The film dwells on the everyday. Once home, Finch washes himself and Dewey, feeds the dog, and then goes to work. He punches a time card, hangs it around his neck, and begins. We see him scanning books – many from the vast library he has painstakingly reassembled – to upload into the memory of the robot he is completing. Then he rests, with the dog beside him.

The event that breaks the routine – the narrative catalyst in a standard plot structure – is the warning of an impending solar storm, which persuades Finch to accelerate his plan: to finish constructing the robot, which he names Jeff, give it a crash course in basic training, and head for San Francisco, where he believes there may still be a chance of survival.

What follows is a classic road movie: memories resurfacing, Jeff's gradual learning that takes the form of a sentimental education, culminating in Finch's death and the symbolic passing of the torch to the robot, who has learned to care for Goodyear. The stylistic choices are once again unsurprising – the miracle of a butterfly, the clear air Finch can finally breathe on his last day, and the dignity of dying well-dressed. The film closes with a dog and a robot walking together across San Francisco's Golden Gate Bridge.

The ending, too, is predictable. And yet the film draws us in; we like it. Certain sensations remain with us: Finch's gentleness, which softens every scene; the sobriety of his gestures, always attentive and measured. Despite the cold neon light and the metallic austerity of the walls, the dimly lit bunker he inhabits feels strangely comforting – at times even pleasant. Perhaps it is the mambo that accompanies his quiet industriousness in that small workshop. The books, too, bring warmth. Almost unnoticed at the beginning of the film, among the volumes Finch scans to upload into the robot's memory are an encyclopedia of dogs, a manual on camper-van driving, and *The Little Prince* – that fable of care and tenderness.

What is most striking, however, is that in this tale of survival, the post-apocalyptic setting remains largely in the background. Even more understated is the true purpose of Finch's project, gradually revealed as Jeff's artificial intelligence evolves – somewhere between binary code and emotion. The robot must not only acquire the skills needed to survive and keep the dog alive; he must also learn to feel and to dream, in order to live with Goodyear. Paradoxically, the future of mankind passes from Finch's hands to Jeff's at the moment when the dog begins to bring the ball back to the robot.

5 Shortened Perspective

In a famous passage from *The Man Without Qualities*, Musil reflects on the human need to give narrative order to one's existence (Mittica 2023). The passage reads as follows:

> And in one of those apparently random and abstract thoughts that so often assumed importance in his life, it struck him that when one is overburdened and dreams of simplifying one's life, the basic law of this life, the law one longs for, is nothing other than that of narrative order, the simple order that enables one to say: "First this happened and then that happened… ." It is the simple sequence of events in which the overwhelmingly manifold nature of things is represented, in a unidimensional order, as a mathematician would say, stringing all that has occurred in space and time on a single thread, which calms us; that celebrated "thread of the story," which is, it seems, the thread of life itself. Lucky the man who can say "when," "before," and "after"! Terrible things may have happened to him, he may have writhed in pain, but as soon as he can tell what happened in chronological order, he feels as contented as if the sun were warming his belly. This is the trick the novel artificially turns to account: Whether the wanderer is riding on the highway in pouring rain or crunching through snow and ice at ten below zero, the reader feels a cozy glow, and this would be hard to understand if this eternally dependable narrative device, which even nursemaids can rely on to keep their little charges quiet, this tried-and-true "foreshortening of the mind's perspective," were not already part and parcel of life itself. Most people relate to themselves as storytellers. They usually have no use for poems, and although the occasional "because" or "in order that" gets knotted into the thread of life, they generally detest any brooding that goes beyond that; they love the orderly sequence of facts because it has the look of necessity, and the impression that their life has a "course" is somehow their refuge from chaos. It now came to Ulrich that he had lost this elementary, narrative mode of thought to which private life still clings, even though everything in public life has already ceased to be narrative and no longer follows a thread, but instead spreads out as an infinitely interwoven surface. (Musil 1995, 122)

Narrative order, says the author, is the law of this life – the order to which we aspire when we feel oppressed and dream of simplicity, a normal order. In their fundamental relation to themselves, almost all human beings are storytellers. Narrative is the means through which we relate to ourselves and, by giving coherent sense to our experience, impose order upon our existence. It is, above all, a temporal order – one that reduces life's overwhelming, even oppressive, variety to a simple sequence.

Yet while recounting existence, Musil also links, almost inadvertently, the need to structure time with the need to find order in space. With the simple touch of a copulative *and*, he opens up the dimension in which we are inevitably exposed – space that, through our capacity to narrate, becomes a map by which we orient ourselves in the world, the story itself serving as a compass.

For a reader attuned to legal culture, the notion of space – necessarily tied to the relational nature of narration – inevitably evokes that of *ethos*. Originally meaning "dwelling" or "place where one lives," the semantics of *ethos* contain the sense of belonging to oneself while simultaneously belonging to what is shared. Hence, it also came to signify the manner in which humans live in relation – as custom and as norm. The suggestion lies here: ethics develops upon this very ground, as the custom of the community, and has always been intertwined with reflection on law, with which it coincides in its original essence.

A few strokes suffice for Musil. With only a handful of words, he allows us to perceive that the variety of life is as real as the story told about it; that threading the line of life together is essential both for belonging to oneself and for orienting oneself within the shared space of human existence – to open oneself to ethics and to the juridical sentiment of being-in-the-world.

Decades of research into narrative within the human and social sciences have reached similar conclusions, as have studies of law as narrative. Narrative practices are always directed toward establishing or re-establishing order – of meanings, of values, of the rules of social coexistence. It is a shared order, one that must be continually reinforced and renegotiated. We tell stories to rediscover a framework of common meaning and, in doing so, to create or strengthen bonds – to mend fractures. Law, too, is part of this narrative fabric.

But Musil goes beyond recognizing the value of narrative construction: he questions and even undermines it. In doing so, he raises a further question – can a story itself serve as a threshold through which to stretch into the realm of limitation?

Describing the narrative order to which almost all people aspire, Musil points out that narration is, more often than not, a well-tested shortening of the perspective of the intellect. For better or worse – whatever the story may be – the narrative provides an ordered framework of meaning that shields us from life itself, from what Simmel would call its continuous transformative movement.

Sense, by contrast, may arise from poetry: a mysterious, alluring, and fearful threshold, stretched toward infinity. Proof of this lies, as Musil notes with irony, in humanity's general indifference to lyric poetry – though he redeems us with that small qualification, "almost all," leaving room for the possibility that human beings can still draw upon sensitive thought. If we understand – if we have access, in some way, to a threshold of sense – it happens poetically, Nancy affirms (1997b).

At this point, as we become aware of having lost our anchorage to the order of the canonical everyday, we happen – along with Ulrich – while our thought stretches out toward a boundless surface.

6 Absence

"The horror of dehumanization does not pass through the representation of pity, but through the staging of the absence of pity," writes Prete (2013, 36), re-reading *In the Penal Colony* by Franz Kafka.

In the story, the space left empty by pity is filled by the fullness of technique, which has completely identified itself with justice and manifests as total power over the human body.

As throughout Kafka's work, the legal machine and its justice are bound to the obsessive guilt of having been born. Amid paradox and metaphor, mystery and vulgarity, the closed doors of the law mark humanity's condemnation simply for existing. Yet while elsewhere the psychological dimension dominates, in *In the Penal Colony*, the relation between the body and the law is more direct and forceful, as it refers to a wound portrayed without mediation – where the justice of law is realized by inscribing itself upon the body of the condemned through the machine, the true protagonist of the tale: "the norm becomes a bloody letter, a wound, the writing of a wound; and the death that follows is the outcome of this physical, total encounter between the body and the law" (Prete 2013, 37).

Described in detail by the officer responsible for its maintenance and operation, the machine is a highly elaborate device used to carry out executions – a feat of engineering in the eyes of its custodian, though clearly cumbersome and precarious.

Its peculiarity lies in the fact that it brings about death over a span of 12 hours, during which the machine (the Harrow) – equipped with needles – gradually engraves the body of the condemned with the words of the sentence imposed on him without trial, of which he knows nothing, just as he knows nothing of his fate. In this way, the condemned man comes to understand the meaning of the judgment inscribed upon his flesh before his death.

> Do you understand the process? The Harrow is starting to write. When it's finished with the first part of the script on the man's back, the layer of cotton wool rolls and turns the body slowly onto its side to give the Harrow a new area. Meanwhile those parts lacerated by the inscription are lying on the cotton wool which, because it has been specially treated, immediately stops the bleeding and prepares the script for a further deepening. Here, as the body continues to rotate, prongs on the edge of the Harrow then pull the cotton wool from the wounds, throw it into the pit, and the Harrow goes to work again. In this way it keeps making the inscription deeper for twelve hours. For the first six hours the condemned man goes on living almost as before. He suffers nothing but pain. After two hours, the felt is removed, for at that point the man has no more energy for screaming. Here at the head of the Bed warm rice pudding is put in this electrically heated bowl. From this the man, if he feels like it, can help himself to what he can lap up with his tongue. No one passes up this opportunity. I don't know of a single one, and I have had a lot of experience. He first loses his pleasure in eating around the sixth hour. I usually kneel down at this point and observe the phenomenon. The man rarely swallows the last bit. He turns it around in his mouth and spits it into the pit. When he does that, I have to lean aside or else he'll get me in the face. But how quiet the man becomes around the sixth hour! The most stupid of them begin to understand. It starts around the eyes and spreads out from there. A look that could tempt one to lie down under the Harrow. Nothing else happens. The man simply begins to decipher the inscription. He purses his lips, as if he is listening. You've seen that it's not easy to figure out the inscription with your eyes, but our man deciphers it with his wounds. True, it takes a lot of work. It requires six hours to complete. But then the Harrow spits him right out and throws him into the pit, where he splashes down into the bloody water and cotton wool. Then the judgment is over, and we, the Soldier and I, quickly bury him. (Kafka 1919, para. 15)

The machine works laboriously to erase what is human. Six hours are required to silence idiocy and vulgarity. During this span, pain too disappears, completing the process of dehumanization, while in the condemned man's new awareness, the law is fulfilled. The 6 hours that follow are the most spectacular and moving. Even the dullest man finally comes to understand, and the beauty of that vision is such that one would be tempted to take his place beneath the Harrow, the officer remarks.

Prete is right to emphasize the complicity between the absence of pity and the reduction of justice to technique. For jurists, needless to say, this is a matter of the greatest importance. Yet the experience of this absence, which opens before us through Kafka's pages and the desolation of his hallucinatory sensibility, moves us not only to reflect on the dehumanization that stems from the distorted relationship between law and technique (and the many other reflections it might provoke), but above all to a renewed feeling of compassion for the human creature condemned without mercy. What involves us is not merely our rejection of the machine, but also our revulsion at the indifference of the condemned man and the soldier, and our reproach toward the explorer who, though refusing to support the officer in resisting the machine's dismantling, ultimately flees without assuming any responsibility. What moves us is pity for human beings when rejection and horror give way to the recognition of another's failings – together with the awareness that we too might be exposed to that same wretchedness.

A similar sensation overtakes us in the final scene of *Pietà* by Kim Ki-duk – a harsh, violent film that pushes human ugliness to its most extreme limits. It is not simply a brutal or spectacular work with psychological undertones, as in Stanley Kubrick's unforgettable *A Clockwork Orange*; in *Pietà*, violence is above all an intimate condition, so painful that it imposes itself upon our sensibility despite our resistance, condemnation, rejection, or even disgust at the acts depicted. Nor does the narrative dimension offer relief: the plot, full of false leads, revolves around the act of revenge and only becomes fully intelligible at the very end. Yet, despite the discomfort the film forces us to endure, we keep watching until the final moment, when – after the protagonist's extreme act – its meaning is revealed as the closing credits begin to roll.

We grasp it through the feeling that takes hold of us: no longer repulsion, rejection, or judgment, but compassion. This is the film's highest, cathartic point. The work happens, and in its unfolding, it opens a threshold that was already held in tension – already awaited – in the title itself. There is no pity within the film; the feeling is reserved solely for the spectator, without whom the work would not come into presence at all, and understanding would remain deserted. The work takes place precisely in this absence.

7 Like a Wave

The tidal motion of refugees,
not the flight of wild geese,
the faces in freight cars,
haggard and coal-eyed,
particularly the peaked stare of children,
the huge bundles crossing bridges, axles creaking
as if joints and bones were audible, the dark stain

spreading on maps whose shapes dissolve their frontiers
the way that corpses melt in a lime-pit or
the bright mulch of autumn is trampled into mud,
and the smoke of a cypress signals Sachsenhausen,
those without trains, without mules or horses,
those who have the rocking chair and the sewing machine
heaped on a human cart, a waggon without horses
for horses have long galloped out of their field
back to the mythology of mercy, back to the cone
of the orange steeple piercing clouds over the lindens
and the stone bells of Sunday over the cobbles,
those who rest their hands on the sides of their carts
as if they were the flanks of mules, and the women
with flint faces, with glazed cheekbones, with eyes
the colour of duck-ponds glazed over with ice,
for whom the year has only one season, one sky:
that of rooks flapping like torn umbrellas,
all have been reduced into a common language,
the homeless, the province-less, to the incredible memory
of apples and clean streams, and the sound of milk
filling the summer churns, where are you from,
what was your district, I know that lake, I know the beer,
and its inns, I believed in its mountains,
now there is a monstrous map that is called Nowhere
and that is where we're all headed, behind it
there is a view called the Province of Mercy,
where the only government is that of the apples
and the only army the wide banners of barley
and its farms are simple, and that is the vision
that narrows in the irises and the dying
and the tired whom we leave in ditches
before they stiffen and their brows go cold
as the stones that have broken our shoes,
as the clouds that grow ashen so quickly after dawn
over palm and poplar, in the deceitful sunrise
of this, your new century. (Walcott 2004)

In *The Prodigal*, Derek Walcott reveals the painful power of his poetry. The tide of refugees moves like a wave, clouding maps and dissolving borders. Heavy burdens cross bridges, defying every conceivable political boundary.

In that dark mass – mud, blood, bone – we see the gaunt faces of men, the fixed expressions of children, and the women's eyes, like frozen ponds. We feel their weariness in the hands resting on the sides of carts piled with what remains of a swept-away everyday life; we sense their fragility in legs that can barely sustain them, almost audible in the creaking of the wooden planks.

Let us read aloud. The poem demands both sound and silence – the time of words and of pauses, of white space. The word is breath itself. Every line moves to a rhythm shaped by waiting.

The refugees are alone. Totally exposed – the homeless, the province-less – they now have only one time and one sky, with no shelter at all. Their only season is that of memory, the incredible remembrance that binds them together in a shared tongue: the memory of apples and clear streams, of milk churning in summer.

Suddenly, the poetic voice – the speaking "I" – changes. It becomes the voices of the refugees themselves, the speech of each one: "where are you from, what was your district, I know that lake, I know the beer, and its inns …" We can hear them, distinguish them within the dark mass, and sense that they are looking back, for ahead lies only darkness and fear: a monstrous map called Nowhere.

Our thoughts grow heavy; the hoarse sound of Walcott's voice rolls like the backwash of the tide. It is there that we are all headed. The land where pity might still have been possible lies behind us – that province where "the only government is that of the apples and the only army the wide banners of barley, and its farms are simple." The same land whose vision narrows in the eyes of those who are dying. And every death is cold and hard – like the sharp stone that cuts the soles of our shoes, halting our steps toward a dawn fated to remain deceitful.

We breathe again, and our landscape is irrevocably changed. It is their time, but it is also our century. We feel ourselves part of that dark tide; every dead body left exhausted in the ditches is the responsibility of us all. We lift our eyes from the page and feel shame – for our privileges, for all that we have failed to do.

8 Lightness

> Hospitality makes one light.
> Hospitality is a silent understanding.
> Truly hospitable, to the very end, is waiting.
> (Jabès 1991)

Hospitality lies at the origin of the social bond and is an inherently juridical relation. As an obligation marked by reciprocity between equals and by responsibility toward those in misfortune, hospitality embodies the fundamental terms of alterity and thirdness that shape the original sense interrogated by the jurist.

To read hospitality through the lens of legal anthropology is a necessary step, yet Jabès's words carry us further.

Lightness. Waiting. Silence.

Silence is one of the great themes of philosophy and art. It is an act of inner gathering, but also of quieting oneself in order to listen to the Other who approaches. Silence weaves a fundamental relation with meaning – a relation we have already considered, including in connection with law (see above, 41).

Jabès (1989, 31) writes:

> Rather than to sense, hold on to the silence which has formed the word. You will learn more about it and about yourself, having both become pure listening.

Silence leads to a sense of limit, opening a threshold toward alterity and allowing us to stretch into a hospitable space. Yet, as Rovatti (1992) aptly observes, silence is above all an exercise – a practice that, from our perspective, is most fruitfully cultivated through our relationship with art:

> Every form of art has its own space for silence: painting, deaf to any commentary, lives in silence yet comes to describe it. Sculpture, mute and silent in spite of itself, jealously guards a cluster of sounds, words, or noises. Poetry, whether written or spoken, lives in silence – broken by words, it lives in the silence of white spaces that cannot be measured, for they can last indefinitely. Music, more than any other art, makes silence its very raw material. (Brunello 2014, 14)

Tracing an arc that links some of the great names of Western music over the past four centuries – from Bach to Cage – Brunello shows how silence gradually becomes a distinct structural element in musical form, revealing that what is commonly perceived as passivity is, in truth, an act of creation:

> In Bach, silence rarely interrupts the natural flow – as if springing from a source – of invention and counterpoint. At most, his silences are breaths, the oxygen that gives natural proportion to the form of his compositions.
>
> Mozart makes of silences and pauses the essential cornerstones that sustain and regulate the pure classicism of his forms, based on the alternation and dialogue of contrasting elements.

> Beethoven finds in the silence of pauses – becoming ever more significant throughout his creative life – a perfect accomplice that allows him to open fissures and suggest paths leading toward infinity.
>
> Schubert turns to silence when he has no more words to express despair, when he can no longer extricate himself from the web of passions, when pain can no longer be sung.
>
> In the modern era, silence in music takes on a structural role, becoming a space of powerful attraction, a field of exploration for composers such as Schoenberg, who sought to place the enduring, age-old elements of human expression alongside a brilliant, though artful, reorganization of sound.
>
> With John Cage, silence finds its true cantor. No one before Cage had seriously considered reversing the roles between sound and silence, nor had anyone regarded silence itself as musical material – as an acceptance of the sounds that already exist. (Brunello 2014, 22–24)

No one explains better than a musician how silence makes it possible to express what cannot be played – to welcome sense in the space of a pause or in the suspension of a note held back in *rubato.*

According to Cage (2015), silence serves to make every other sound in the world resonate, revealing the dimension of coexistence – the horizon of being-in-common that manifests itself to the jurist who listens attentively to the manifold voices not only of human beings but of all living things, of nature itself.

Silence is the art most cherished by those who attend to sense, placing themselves in that state of waiting which, for Jabès, is precisely the attentive readiness through which silent hospitality becomes understanding. Truly hospitable, in the fullest sense, is waiting itself, for one becomes the guest of another only by learning to dwell within alterity, accepting its irreducible element – by being able to attend to the Other, to remain in waiting without closing oneself off, allowing sense to come, to take shape, and to reach outward again.

And finally, lightness. Why does hospitality make us light? Such a direct statement deserves an equally direct response: hospitality makes us light because, in encountering the Other, we fulfill our humanity. Not because this encounter is free from unease or untouched by pain – far from it. To stand truly before the Other is to stand before a mirror that reflects our own incompleteness through something foreign, destined to remain so – distant and potentially hostile. Yet we feel lighter, for we have at last come home to ourselves. We can exist.

9 The Old Man and the Young Man

Let us conclude our work by rereading a fragment by Francesco Carnelutti on the art of law, in which the jurist's condition is explicitly that of one who interrogates sense through the complexity of feeling, striving toward an understanding that goes beyond the knowledge of science. In Carnelutti's praxis, as Cananzi (2017b, xvii) rightly observes, we discern the spirit of the artisan jurist, who reveals "the enchantment that law can open when the jurist is capable of believing in what cannot be immediately seen and listens to what the work itself says [...] the enchantment of measure."

> Is this, then, law? And is this the jurist who claims to know what law is? In the end, he knows nothing definite. He speaks, in short, not as a scholar but as a poet.
>
> It is precisely here that the difference lies between my youth and my old age as a jurist. The young man believed he knew; the old man knows that he does not know. And when knowledge is joined by the knowledge of not knowing, then science becomes poetry. The young man was content with the scientific concept of law; the old man feels that within that concept its impulse, its drama, and thus its truth, are lost. The young man sought the sharp outlines of definition; the old man prefers the nuances of comparison. The young man believed only in what he could see; the old man now believes only in what cannot be seen. The young man stood on the left; the old man has crossed to the right side of the bridge. And, finally, to represent that land where men love one another and, in loving, achieve freedom, even poetry is scarcely enough; the jurist would wish to be a musician, so that men might hear its enchantment. (Carnelutti 2017, 18–19)

"An art that is, is not" (Kiefer 2011).

Carnelutti is fully aware of this. His very writing confirms it – a living word and a work at once. What strikes us most is precisely this form, revealing the condition of the man and jurist in constant dialogue with his own limit, and thus open to the alterity–thirdness of law, to the relation with the other person – a Thou – to whom he entrusts the chiaroscuro of his lifelong meditation on the question that haunts every jurist: "What is law?"

It is not only Carnelutti's vision of poetic understanding beyond science, or of music beyond the mathematics of law, that moves us – it is also his way of speaking.

What astonishes us most is the gentleness of tone, attuned to the calm voice of old age; the use of simple, familiar words that everyone can understand, reminding us that law belongs to all; and, not least, the rhythm. The alternating perspectives of the young and the old jurist create a threshold where patient, humble thought takes form – a thought composed more of shades and silences than of certainties.

Carnelutti shows us that thinking that feels is not self-serving – it knows how to attend.

When asked why art, Kiefer (2011) replies that nothing escapes art. Art is the most authentic mediator of reality, where reality coincides with sense infinitely present in the sign. What is real is what remains invisible, unsayable: only this mystery is real, while the reality we take for such is but illusion – mere image.

Kiefer bears witness that the more knowledge one acquires, the more the doors of the unknown are flung open; that form becomes artistic when it allows one to draw from the work something different from what is evident. Carnelutti shows that the old jurist reaches toward what he cannot see, precisely because he knows the existence of a limit and is aware that only in this way can he restore to juridical form the enchantment of measure in the service of being-in-common.

For both, the encounter with life unfolds on the terrain of mystery, resolutely oriented toward the discovery of forms as thresholds in which to stretch, limits to inhabit, and boundaries to share. There seems to be no difference between a jurist and any other artist in the sensibility at work in their search for sense. Nor, ideally, should there be any difference in the quality of the form that sense assumes, if the work – whether a legal norm or another creation – is made-with-art, if it allows the being of the threshold to come forth.

Some lines from Ingeborg Bachmann's poem *Bohemia Lies by the Sea*, written in 1964, are quoted by Kiefer (2011) as a work whose presence has been constant in his life. Read in this light, they appear as more than a suggestion about the art of law – an art of boundaries:

> If a word here borders on me, I'll let it border.
> If Bohemia still lies by the sea, I'll believe in the sea again.
> And believing in the sea, thus I can hope for land.
> If it's me, then it's anyone, for he's as worthy as me.
> [...] I still border on a word and on another land,
> I border, like little else, on everything more and more.
> (Bachmann 2006)

AFTERWORD

How Law Thinks, or "Pensif" Law

In one of his most recent contributions, François Jullien reflects on "how literature thinks," taking as his point of departure Balzac's *Sarrasine* (Jullien 2025). In the novella, the Marchioness Béatrix de Rochefide is told, in a complete and exhaustive manner, both the story of a failed and lost love and the turbulent life of an old gentleman encountered at a reception – a specter of the youthful Adonis he once was. Balzac closes the novella with the words: "… Et la marquise resta pensive."

Jullien asks: why does the Marchioness remain – depending on how one chooses to translate the French term – "pensive," "thoughtful," "thinking"? What is it about the story she has heard that fails to satisfy her and instead leaves her in this state?

Jullien's first observation is that this pensiveness arises from having been confronted with a life story – with life itself. It is precisely life that "produces thought," rendering not only Balzac's narrative but literature as a whole thinking. It is life that causes the Marchioness – and all of us, with her and like her – to remain always thinking, thoughtful, pensive (Jullien 2025, 7).

M. Paola Mittica's beautiful book partakes in this state of being *pensif*, which – through literature and other forms of artistic expression, as fruitfully practiced within Law and Humanities studies – finds its privileged field of inquiry in law. As the author writes: "Literature comes into play where science fails. It possesses the freedom needed to travel paths other than rationality, giving space also to what cannot be said" (see below, 106), the unsaid that belongs precisely to the sense of juridicality: that ensemble of forms (in the strong esthetic sense) that are "thresholds in which to stretch oneself in order to grasp the reasons for being-in-common" (see above, 28).

Today, as yesterday and as tomorrow, the science of law finds itself obliged to reckon with this *pensif*: not so much with changes in juridicality as with the magmatic nature of life itself, which both orients and demands those changes. Consequently, legal science must calibrate juridical measure in relation to life as it flows inexorably onward,[1] thereby constituting a problem that must continually be thought and rethought.

1 See B.-C. Han (2017b) on the notion of *quan* as a symbol whose range of meanings confers a distinctive character on the Chinese idea of law. *Quan* lacks any definitive, absolute, or immutable trait. Originally, it refers to the weight that oscillates on a steelyard. In this

 | HTTPS://DOI.ORG/10.1163/9789004757714-006

Today, more than ever – and precisely with an eye to the future – legal science must bring to light that very "thinking that feels," which Mittica frames with precision. Although this has always been part of the jurist's approach to life (as the entire history of legal philosophy amply demonstrates),[2] today it can no longer remain implicit or be acquired solely through practical experience. Rather, it must be mediated and metabolized, for it enables familiarity with that highly peculiar phenomenon that is law – about which Giuseppe Capograssi's observation holds true (1962, 6): the more one tries to grasp it, the more it slips through one's fingers.[3]

In the three chapters that make up the book – enriched in this edition by an important fourth stage in the journey presented here as an appendix – Mittica offers decisive support in this work of unveiling. She guides us toward an understanding of a form of thought – juridical thought – that "feels" and that must feel. But what does juridical thought feel, or what should it feel?

It feels the "reasonableness of feeling" (see above, 67), indispensable for holding together "being-in-common" as a shared third space, where the interrogation of meaning takes place "before the Other – whether another human being, a Thou, or any other living being" (see above, 23), employing the tools of that sapiential craftsmanship that constitutes the "art of law," at whose center stands the claim: "*reck* of being-in-common is their aim" (see above, 62).

But how can thought be *pensif*? How can thought feel?

Certainly, if, when we speak of thought – and of juridical thought in particular – we have in mind that stereotypical caricature of modernity that informs common discourse, then a *pensif* thought, a thought that feels, is impossible and, in any case, useless: impossible because sensibility eludes abstract, *more geometrico* reasoning; useless because it is relegated to that impurity of human action – too human – that "scientific" science ought to purge, or at least avoid.

From thought thus reduced and understood – from so-called technical, purely scientific thought (see above, 29) – one demands certain and invariant answers, of the kind that perhaps only algorithmization can ambiguously promise to those whom, recalling Eco's metaphor (2001), we might call "integrated" types, obsessed with having ideas that are always clear and distinct.

---

initial sense, *quan* means to weigh and to balance: it has no fixed or final position but is instead mobile, adjustable, and provisional, much like the sliding weight of a balance.

2 See in particular François Ost (1999, 2018), which aptly illustrate the cultural vitality and theoretical rigor of contemporary legal philosophy.

3 See also Capograssi (1962, 237): "Nothing is more necessary to the life of law than science, and nothing is more necessary to science than the life of law."

Yet, it is precisely this that ultimately constitutes a fine challenge, one to which Mittica's pages open the door not only to doubt but, above all, to deconstruction, leading beyond the threshold of the apparent necessity of certainty and toward what the author, echoing Jullien, calls "true life": a life that "resists obscuration by the constraining apparatus of civilization" (see above, 10).

What does this entail? What is the challenge of "thinking that feels," and of those who reclaim pensiveness for thought? It entails, for example, coming to terms with modernity and with what it has produced; for law and legal science, it means coming to terms with affectivity – which Mittica clarifies so well in these pages – too hastily relegated to other domains. Jullien, too, observes and develops this point, bringing to light that "logic of existence" (Jullien 2025, 123) with which law and legal science are imbued. As Jullien notes in the pages already mentioned, one must "recover the paradox that philosophy has abandoned to religion" (*ibid.*, 125), namely the paradox of the "tension" and "torsion" that life itself imposes upon the living (*ibid.*, 124).

All the more so because today – and even more so tomorrow – the jurist has no use for a mode of thought informed solely by clarity and distinction, and therefore intent on filing away affective sensibility. The issues he is called upon to unravel have become so complex, and the systems – at once juridical, political, economic, and religious – within which he must act are so intricately articulated.

Mittica is therefore right – as François Ost had already perceptively noted in his intense preface to the Italian edition, and now again in this one (see above, X-XVIII) – to evoke a sensitive form of thought, sensitive precisely because it is "incarnate": concrete without being mere praxis, universal without being abstract, common without being assimilationist. How can a form of thought attain such stature? By aiming at that "intimate universal" – as Jullien (2025, 94 ff.) calls it – which Mittica brings to light in these pages, where the incarnation of law confronts the question of its limits, just as the body comes to know itself by encountering what does not belong to it, and continues to recognize itself by becoming familiar with its own parts, with the intimate affectivity through which it is expressed.

Like literature (and even before literature),[4] law thinks the concrete intimacy of the human, which becomes embodied each time in a particular person, yet still constitutes a universal. *Pensif* law works on the history of this "intimate universal," synthesizing freedom and obligation, rule and action, order and magmatic flux. Legal science needs this *pensif* form of thought

4 Forgetting or underestimating this has had significant consequences for theories of law.

because, otherwise, it would tend to oppose freedom and obligation, rule and action, order and magmatic flux, thus outlining an anti-vital law and reconstructing it no longer on being-in-common as de-coinciding alterity,[5] but on the coinciding egoity of those who have the power to compel action by limiting freedom, to impose rules by directing action, to establish their own order by arresting magmaticity.

Such a legal science is that of a "law that does not feel": it thinks, not by chance, in terms of abstract (not intimate) universals, in definitions rather than qualifications, conceptually and through concepts. It proves itself incapable – echoing Mittica's words – of a "good use of law," anesthetized to the human, both because it has been deprived of affective sensibility and, no less importantly, because it has been deprived of an aesthetics of law and confined to the "autistic logic of juridical representation – cut off from reality," capable of using law only as "a mere mechanical application, thereby losing sight of its purpose" (see above, 29).

By contrast, legal science must be capable of "opening concepts and placing them in tension with what most resists them, testing them against what precisely escapes the concept" (Jullien 2025, 119), that is, that "tear in the eye of the law" (Hugo 2000), which gives warmth, flavor, and taste to the juridical and to its affective rationality, to its incarnate sensibility.

These pages have accompanied and guided the fascinated reader along an intense path, revealing how law thinks and, to echo once more Mittica's words, is constructed in the hope "that the jurist may learn the art of listening and giving voice to the juridical sense-sentiment as it arises, so as to understand and give form to the most just measure" (see above, 66).

Is this not the task of the jurist and of legal science – to place the weight that measures in the right position on the scales of justice?

Then life will be respected, and the power to say and to do will affirm not a privilege for oneself but a right for all and for each, thanks to *au jurist (qui et quand reste) pensif.*

Daniele M. Cananzi
Professor of Philosophy of Law at the University Mediterranea of Reggio Calabria, and Director of CRED – Research Center for the Aesthetics of Law

5 On the dimension of de-coincidence, also in the sense used here, see Jullien (2018b).

APPENDIX

The Last Pagan on Earth: A Tribute to Cormac McCarthy

> When this world which reason has created is carried off at last it will take reason with it. And it will be a long time coming back. (*Stella Maris* 140)

1 McCarthy's Last, Precious Pages

Cormac McCarthy is one of the major authors of our time and needs no introduction. He passed away on June 13, 2023, at the age of 89, leaving an indelible mark on all who have read him. His prose is dry and stark, shaped by an uncompromising vision of human misery – at times almost unbearable – yet also compassionate and imbued with a rare poetry.

His last two novels, published in 2022, *The Passenger* and *Stella Maris*, represent a project on which McCarthy had long been working and may rightly be considered his testament. More precisely, the two works – complementary and parallel – form a diptych telling in two voices a single story: that of the siblings Robert and Alicia Western.

In *The Passenger*, the primary voice is Bobby's. The title invokes the metaphor of the missing passenger from a submerged airplane – a mystery that triggers the protagonist's flight and remains unresolved throughout. As it becomes clearer the further one reads, this narrative device is not intended to construct a plot, which is deliberately unstructured. The corpse that is never found functions instead as a symbolic mechanism pointing to a kind of failed death, a desertion of one's post, a body lost in the depths of the sea with no further contact with the surface of the world. It reflects Bobby's feeling for his sister, who died by suicide – one of the radiating cores of McCarthy's story – and leads us into the mystery of a form of understanding that seeks to extend beyond rationality. The journey the protagonist undertakes begins as a flight but ultimately becomes an initiation.

Stella Maris is the name of a psychiatric hospital – a space at the margins of the system. Here, the conventional is suspended, personalities proliferate, language is deconstructed, and visions take on increasingly abstract forms. But *Stella Maris* is also one of the names of the Virgin Mary and of the North Star, both symbols of guidance – of someone or something in whom one might

 | HTTPS://DOI.ORG/10.1163/9789004757714-007

place one's trust. Alicia's decision to live there until the end of her days is bound up with all this, and more. The voice of *Stella Maris* is hers: she speaks with the psychoanalyst responsible for her care in a dialogue that comprises the entire novel.

Just as the North Star guides navigators, for Bobby *Stella Maris* is Alicia. Both live in the rupture of the world's canvas, with the difference that Alicia has always been aware of it, while her brother tends to retreat from understanding. In *Stella Maris*, she tells her psychoanalyst:

> Bobby wasn't happy about any of this. I'd stopped talking about it. But by then he'd given up all pretense of an interest in the verity of life on the other side of the glass and he was only interested in how to get rid of it. And by then I wasn't all that sure that I wanted to. Get rid of it.
> *Why?*
> Because I knew what my brother did not. (*Stella Maris* 156)

Like other works previously considered in the context of Law and Humanities, this new text contains no explicit reflection on law. The only references to law, justice, and injustice serve to describe feelings of guilt, anger, or love.

The great value of these two novels lies in the force with which they draw us into a dimension of limit, calling all our intelligences to account before life – to grasp those possible forms of our existence to which we cannot gain access and, faced with the failure of our idea of progress and the world we have devastated, to return, perhaps, to reflecting on what our species should truly understand by growth. In this way, they call ethics into question, an indispensable premise for restoring to law its role as a human instrument for seeking sense, even in what cannot be conceived, and for safeguarding the living in all its forms.

2 They Weren't Good Enough

In McCarthy's eyes, the contemporary world has imploded. Western humanity finds itself leaning over the abyss dug by its own idea of progress, whose only outcome has been the discovery, on the one hand, of the human creature's unchanged capacity for destruction and, on the other, of the limits of our ability to understand – a limit marked by a beyond whose existence can only be sensed. It is as if he were telling us, while we run blindly toward the end, that the one thing our ingenuity has managed to do is expose us to self-destruction without ever truly opening our minds.

> In the end, she had said, there will be nothing that cannot be simulated. And this will be the final abridgment of privilege. This is the world to come. Not some other. The only alternate is the surprise in those antic shapes burned into the concrete.
>
> The ages of men stretching grave to grave. (*The Passenger* 382)

It is Bobby who reports Alicia's words: she had foreseen that by pushing technical rationality ever further and relying solely on it, nothing would remain of human beings but their graves.

What most forcefully articulates the critique of twentieth-century history is the way the Western siblings' biography intersects with the development of the atomic bomb:

> [...] anyone who doesn't understand that the Manhattan Project is one of the most significant events in human history hasn't been paying attention. It's up there with fire and language. (*Stella Maris* 64)

Their parents had met at the Oak Ridge Laboratory and later lived in Los Alamos. Alicia and Bobby's father was among the nuclear physicists involved in the Manhattan Project, and he had seen Trinity and Ivy Mike flare. It is not by chance that his name is *Western*:

> Western fully understood that he owed his existence to Adolf Hitler. That the forces of history which had ushered his troubled life into the tapestry were those of Auschwitz and Hiroshima, the sister events that sealed forever the fate of the West. (*The Passenger* 165)

The Western siblings are devastated children, just as the world of Western culture is devastated. McCarthy makes them the threshold from which to confront the horror of the history of the idea of "human civilization" imposed by the West.[1]

But this is not all. It is the 1980s. The major scientific developments of the twentieth century – the theory of relativity, quantum mechanics, the uncertainty principle, among others – had already dismantled the foundations of the modern world, throwing open the coordinates of what until then had been imagined as the only dimension of life: a unilinear time and a three-dimensional space. This marks the end of determinism, which – although

1 In *The Passenger*, McCarthy also connects the protagonists' personal story with other tragic events in American history, such as Vietnam or Kennedy's assassination. In one of his

initially confined to the awareness of a scientific elite – nevertheless erodes, quietly and underground, the belief that the reality one inhabits is the true one (or even the only true one), stirring the suspicion of another realm just as real, though dark and impenetrable.

"They weren't good enough," says Bobby, referring to the figures who shaped the history of twentieth-century science. (*The Passenger* 154)

Bobby would have been a brilliant physicist, but he left university. He prefers to flee the scientific world and, after competing in France as a race-car driver, now works as a diver – facing, with every descent, his terror of darkness and depth.

Alicia is an absolute mathematical genius. She chooses to have herself admitted to the psychiatric hospital Stella Maris because she is schizophrenic and unable to adapt: she has a mind that exceeds the system, consuming the world with extreme rapidity while longing for a reality she knows exists beyond knowledge.

What the two siblings experience is a disorientation that reveals an irreversible fracture in the trust placed in human rationality. It is merely verbal intelligence, McCarthy writes. It cannot push beyond the wall of a world created by language – the only world it can comprehend.

> [...] when you're talking about intelligence you're talking about number. A claim that the mathless are quick to frown upon. It's about calculation and the nature of calculation. Verbal intelligence will only take you so far. There is a wall there, and if you don't understand numbers you won't even see the wall. (*Stella Maris* 71)

In *Stella Maris*, speaking with Dr. Cohen about the unconscious, mathematics, and language, Alicia recalls the discovery she made as a child about equations after a conversation with her father:

> I understood – really understood – that the equations were not a supposition of the form whose life was confined to the symbols on the page which described them but that they were there before my eyes. In actuality. They were in the paper, the ink, in me. The universe. Their invisibility could never speak against

conversations with Kline – the ambiguous private investigator who is supposed to help him disappear – after listening to the extremely detailed reconstruction of one of the hypotheses about Kennedy's murder, Western asks how that story concerns him. "This country is your problem," Kline replies. "It is?" Bobby answers. "It's not?" (Kline) "I'd have to think about it" (Bobby) (*The Passenger* 336).

> them or their being. Their age. Which was the age of reality itself. Which was itself invisible and always had been. (*Stella Maris* 87–88)

Numbers are sensed, felt:

> All I can tell you is that I like numbers. I like their shapes and their colors and their smells and the way they taste. (*Stella Maris* 87)

Beyond the wall of the world created by language and human rationality lies a reality that emerges through mathematics – a reality that verbal intelligence alone cannot grasp. The same applies, as we shall see, to music, which, Alicia notes, "is not a language. It has no reference to anything other than itself" (*Stella Maris* 39). For McCarthy, this elsewhere is the territory of the unconscious. In it resides the capacity to confront what is inexplicable and alien: the horrific and the compassionate that dwell within human beings. Upon it depends the possibility of living sentimentally.

The unconscious surfaces in the Western siblings' experience in order to confront the blindness of science, to mark the limits of human rationality, and to open up new forms of understanding with which to face fear, happiness, and love: "exquisitely novelistic problems," Alicia might ironically remark (Lagioia 2023b, para. 15).

It follows that the third figure of absolute importance, in both *The Passenger* and *Stella Maris*, is the Thalidomide Kid, Alicia's second personality, who will also, significantly, speak with Bobby once the latter is ready to receive him.

The Thalidomide Kid is likewise a child of the horror produced by Western science. He takes the form of a man born deformed because of thalidomide, a German drug that, between the 1950s and 1960s, was also prescribed to pregnant women, causing severe fetal malformations and the birth of more than 10,000 children with genetic deformities worldwide.[2]

He is a creature who visits Alicia almost daily in the period before her institutionalization.

While in *Stella Maris*, the Kid appears only as a theme within the therapeutic narrative, in *The Passenger*, he reaches his fullest expression. The very form of the novel – structured in chapters that alternate even typographically – is conceived to develop in parallel Alicia's story, crystallized in the present of an anonymous rented room, where she struggles with what emerges from within

2 There are numerous scientific articles that document the seriousness of the effects of thalidomide, as well as journalistic reports recounting this scandal. Without going into detail, see Rigby (2007).

herself without being able to control it, and Bobby's story, who, several years after her death, wanders confused and devastated among other survivors in the marginal America so dear to McCarthy, while evading investigators seeking to clarify the mystery of the plane crash and the missing body.

The Kid is always surprising. At each visit, he proposes topics, riddles, and little performances as improbable as his disjointed, incongruent, and enigmatic language. Alicia is irritated by him, though she recognizes that at times something in the Thalidomide Kid's outbursts would merit understanding:

> It was mostly nonsense. Interspersed with comments that were pretty interesting. Sometimes. But mostly talk that you might characterize as schizoid. Klang associations. Rhyming. None of which echoed my own interior life. (*Stella Maris* 128)

The young mathematician cannot live within the farce. Because she understands numbers, she sees the wall – and the Kid, as he repeatedly asserts, is working for her, revealing what others, those who remain on the surface of the world, could never even begin to approach:

> Listen, Ducklescence [...]. You will never know what the world is made of. The only thing that's certain is that it's not made of the world. As you close upon some mathematical description of reality you can't help but lose what is being described. Every inquiry displaces what is addressed. A moment in time is a fact, not a possibility. The world will take your life. But above all and lastly the world does not know that you are here. You think that you understand this. But you don't. Not in your heart you don't. If you did you would be terrified. And you're not. Not yet. And now, good night. (*The Passenger* 128)

> *These beings that come to entertain you but they're not very good at it. Entertain. Distract. What do you think it is that they're supposed to be doing?*
> I don't know what it is that they're supposed to be doing. It's all lame beyond words.
> *You must have some notion of what it is that they want.*
> They want to do something with the world that you haven't thought of. They want to set it at question.
> *Why would they?*
> Because that's who they are. What they are. If you just wanted an affirmation of the world you wouldn't need to conjure up weird beings. (*Stella Maris* 23)

Bobby lacks his sister's clarity, nor does he wish to confront the problems of a supposed elsewhere. He is a restless man who moves convulsively through a life of fragments, driven solely by his love for Alicia: the unconsummated love of two lovers, which she would have lived fully, but which Bobby refuses – denying happiness to both and cultivating within himself a deep sense of guilt.

> I thought that the fact that it wasn't acceptable wasn't really our problem. I knew that he loved me. He was just afraid. I'd known this was coming for a long time. There was no place else for me to go. (*Stella Maris* 164)

> We were like the last on earth. We could choose to join the beliefs and practices of the millions of dead beneath our feet or we could begin again. Did he really have to think about it? [...] I told him that I wanted to have his child.
> [...]
> Look. It's no good you repeating these things to me as if to limn the horror and the lunacy of them. You can't see the world I see. You can't see through these eyes. You never will. (*Stella Maris* 166)

Some have wished to see in this love between siblings an act of revolt against the established order – aimed not only at breaking the taboo of incest itself, but at breaking the fact that the incest is between brother and sister rather than parent and child. It appears as a legitimate protest, however self-destructive, against the empire of the fathers – the demiurges of modernity – found also in other contexts.[3]

However, Alicia's words direct our gaze toward a still more primordial form of love – one that employs incest to lead us back to foundational myths. This love recalls the figure of Dionysus preserved in the Orphic tradition: the god who is both male and female, who seems to take shape in the fusion between the two siblings toward which Alicia strives, evoking once again, in this different expression, the same ambition to know beyond the limit. Of Dionysus, Colli writes:

> [With Dionysus] life appears as wisdom, while remaining trembling life: this is the mystery. [...] Dionysus is born from a glance upon all of life: but how can one look at all of life at once? This is the arrogance of knowing: if one lives, one

3 One example is the young mathematician's decision to change her given name from Alice to Alicia. This is not a meaningless detail. Alice rejects her father's choice to give his children the names of the two characters used in scientific problems presented in narrative form – that is, Bob and Alice (*Stella Maris* 28). Irony? An inability to look beyond his own work? Lack of affection? Understanding parenthood as yet another experiment?

> is inside a certain life, but wanting to be inside all of life at once – this is what summons Dionysus [...]. (Colli 1990, 15)

Alicia and Bobby are fused together. The difference is that she would wager on the possibility of going beyond the world – of beginning again, almost giving rise to a new species, a "world at once antique and never to be" (*The Passenger* 381); whereas he is not (yet) capable of overcoming the constraints of convention.

Bobby does not possess Alicia's daring excess. And it is precisely this that makes him the tragic hero of the two novels: the man stretched within the limit, the survivor, the passenger.

Although consumed by guilt and by the desire to be re-united with Alicia, whose excess led her to take her own life, Bobby continues to live, gradually maturing his evolutionary task. It is an unconscious process that unfolds throughout the novel. Among his choices, the most revealing is his decision to become a salvage diver. Bobby does not like descending into cold and darkness. The depth terrifies him; yet he still plunges down, even against his will, to search and retrieve. The metaphor is powerful. Deep waters evoke an unknown and treacherous environment, and at the same time a fluid one, in which every movement is possible – as it once was for everyone in the maternal womb. Those with experience of diving know this sensation, and also know that the deeper one goes, the more logical capacities fade, making room for other resources. It is one of McCarthy's ways of tracing Bobby's path toward a different form of understanding, whose North Star is *Stella Maris*.

3 The Kekulé Problem

The unconscious is therefore a central dimension in the two novels. On the one hand, it recounts the repression of a collective trauma that barely conceals the horror hidden within our civilization – the same civilization capable of provoking two world wars and constructing the atomic bomb, which was duly dropped. On the other hand, the unconscious reclaims its status as an original cognitive resource, opening onto a reality that exceeds the world constructed by verbal intelligence.

It is this second dimension that most deeply shapes the reflection developed in the two novels.

In the only essay he published in 2017, *The Kekulé Problem*,[4] McCarthy argues that the unconscious is a biological system that evolved within the human species, governing and preserving life for millions of years – long before the appearance of language, which surfaced roughly one hundred thousand years ago:

> One hundred thousand years is pretty much an eyeblink. But two million years is not. This is, rather loosely, the length of time in which our unconscious has been organizing and directing our lives. And without language you will note. (McCarthy 2017, para. 16)

As both McCarthy in the essay and his young protagonist in *Stella Maris* argue, language must have emerged in the brain like a virus. It would have insinuated itself into the less developed areas of the brain and, because it enabled an articulation and differentiation of sounds into countless variants for naming reality, proved so useful that it gradually took hold of the human mind – reducing it, in time, to reasoning only through language and with only one part of the brain.

In this way, language likely circumscribed the boundaries of our world, becoming the only means of accessing it at the level of knowledge.

---

4 This essay was published in *Nautilus*, a wide-ranging scientific journal that maintains close ties with researchers and projects associated with the Santa Fe Institute, where McCarthy was active for nearly twenty years, working closely with scientists, including those from the hard sciences. The experience of the Santa Fe Institute presents a particularly interesting feature. The Institute is dedicated to the study of complex systems and to the development of the so-called "Third Culture," understood as a multidisciplinary and integrated approach aimed at addressing twenty-first-century challenges by bringing together researchers from across scientific fields as well as from literature, as in McCarthy's case.

Introducing the novelist's essay, David Krakauer – an evolutionary biologist and president of the Santa Fe Institute, a position he already held in 2017 – writes: "Over the last two decades, Cormac and I have been discussing the puzzles and paradoxes of the unconscious mind. Foremost among them is the fact that the very recent and 'uniquely' human capability of near-infinite expressive power, arising through a combinatorial grammar, is built on the foundations of a far more ancient animal brain. How have these two evolutionary systems become reconciled? Cormac expresses this tension as a deep suspicion, perhaps even contempt, that the primeval unconscious feels toward the upstart, conscious language. In this article, Cormac explores this idea through processes of dream and infection. It is a discerning and wide-ranging exploration of ideas and challenges that our research community has only recently dared to begin addressing through complexity science" (McCarthy 2017, para. 1).

> But you have to understand what the advent of language was like. The brain had done pretty well without it for quite a few million years. The arrival of language was like the invasion of a parasitic system. Co-opting those areas of the brain that were the least dedicated. The most susceptible to appropriation. (*Stella Maris* 177)
> [...]
> *Troubling words. But I think you've suggested that the advent of language, aside from the enormous value of it, was disruptive.*
> Very disruptive. Of a piece with its value. Creative destruction. All sorts of talents and skills must have been lost. Mostly communicative. But also things like navigation and probably even the richness of dreams. In the end this strange new code must have replaced at least part of the world with what can be said about it. Reality with opinion. Narrative with commentary.
> *And sanity with madness, don't forget.*
> Yes. I won't. (*Stella Maris* 178)

For McCarthy, the essential point is that the unconscious functions better than language. Language may formulate the most difficult questions, but the answers arise from the unconscious – and in a non-verbal, enigmatic mode, most often surfacing in dreams to tell us more, and in a more cryptic way, because it wants us to think about them:[5]

> I suppose that sometimes the unconscious will keep working on certain dreams, revising them, hoping you'll get it. (*Stella Maris* 82)

This is what dreams are for. The problem is that we struggle to decipher them.

On this side of the world, everything is language – the older form that arises from the practice of counting, and the verbal form which, when it becomes writing, definitively completes the process of disembodying the world.[6] But,

5 Freud and Jung are explicitly cited several times in the novels; for a discussion from this perspective, see Dufourmantelle (2024).

6 Regarding the origin of language, McCarthy limits himself to pointing out its capacity to colonize the human brain, without identifying its underlying premise. In his review of *Stella Maris*, Nicola Lagioia (2023b, para. 14) offers a possible answer by drawing on Ginzburg's thesis concerning the transition from oral to written culture: "When, in sixth-century Athens, the transcription of the Homeric poems – until then transmitted orally – was perfected, something decisive happened. What had been voices, gestures, bodies, community, matter was uprooted, so to speak, from its culture medium, and this is fairly clear. What is not reflected upon enough is that this uprooting is also a dis-embodiment; it pushes to the extreme the process of abstraction that had begun earlier. 'Texts, maps, and coins imply abstraction,' writes Ginzburg. With writing, the language-text becomes definitively abstract,

indeed, there is also a beyond-language which, for McCarthy, belongs to the unconscious.

> The core question is not how you do math but how does the unconscious do it. How is it that it's demonstrably better at it than you are? (*Stella Maris* 102)

In his essay, McCarthy (2017, para. 5) recounts how his colleagues at the Santa Fe Institute confirmed that the unconscious mind can solve mathematical problems without passing through the structures of mathematics. "My friend George Zweig calls this the Night Shift," he notes, and other colleagues agreed that such a phenomenon is possible. Mathematical language is needed to advance reasoning – to provide stability, continuity, and causality in solving complex problems – but the generation of a single mathematical insight may occur in the mind without passing through mathematical forms, even though those forms remain its infrastructure.

There is more. Language – even mathematical language – risks slowing down or distorting the broader understanding guided by the unconscious.

As Bobby recalls of Alicia:

> She saw everything differently. She would figure something out and then half the time she couldn't explain to you how she'd done it. [...] She didn't draw pictures. She hardly even did calculations. (*The Passenger* 286)

Alicia herself explains to the Kid why it is important to resort to writing as little as possible:

> What you write down becomes fixed. It takes on the constraints of any tangible entity. It collapses into a reality estranged from the realm of its creation. It's a marker. A roadsign. You have stopped to get your bearings, but at a price. You'll never know where it might have gone if you'd left it alone to go there. [...] I don't know how one does mathematics. I don't know that there is a way. The idea is always struggling against its own realization. Ideas come with an innate skepticism, they don't just go barreling ahead. And these doubts have their origin in the same world as the idea itself. And that's not something you really

invisible, capable of being laid down (and reproduced) identically on any medium. But where does the process begin? Where does the idea (to use Alicia/McCarthy's words) 'that one thing can be another' originate? Ginzburg again writes: 'It has been suggested that the earliest evidence of this kind of abstraction is linked to the act of counting.'"

> have access to. [...] Once a mathematical conjecture is formalized into a theory [...] [i]t has in fact begun to look like a tool. (*The Passenger* 297)

McCarthy's point, in other words, is that although language is a powerful and useful instrument for confronting and explaining problems, the actual process of thought is largely the work of the unconscious.

To the question "What does language represent for the unconscious?" one could say that language functions as a device for giving shape to a formless body of knowledge that is the unconscious:

> The log of knowledge or information contained in the brain of the average citizen is enormous. But the form in which it resides is largely unknown. [...] When you pause to reflect and say: "Let me see. How can I put this," your aim is to resurrect an idea from this pool of we-know-not-what and give it a linguistic form so that it can be expressed. (McCarthy 2017, para. 17–18)

The point is that language, in describing reality, creates a limited world – one circumscribed by its own description, the only world that becomes "conceivable" – whereas the range of our thought is far more extensive.

It is significant that Bobby's eloquence, brilliant at first, gradually diminishes as he approaches his truest existential condition, until he makes almost no use of words. After all, as his friend Sheddan says:

> And what are we? Ten percent biology and ninety percent nightrumor. (*The Passenger* 378)

4 Literature as a Resource

Literature comes into play where science fails. It possesses the freedom needed to travel paths other than rationality, giving space also to what cannot be said.

In the form McCarthy gives to the two novels, literature appears above all as a way of turning against itself the order that would emerge from a conventional use of language and narrative construction. Lagioia (2023a) notes that Alicia's schizophrenia is an ideal narrative device for staging the most turbulent of relationships between the unconscious and language. Once the bulkhead of mental linearity is broken, the unconscious erupts, and language collapses upon itself:

> literary art is language used against itself, expressive language against functional language, perception against information, and finally an attempt (perpetually failed, continually necessary) at a language without language. Literature, when it becomes irreducible to other linguistic forms, speaks without speaking. (Lagioia 2023a, para. 32)

When literature "speaks without speaking," it becomes poetry. In this lies the intensity of McCarthy's writing.

The long descriptions that punctuate the pages of *The Passenger* do not limit themselves to stating the explicit. They also convey the invisible: the suffering of Bobby and Alicia, their secret, their dark truth. Saying one thing through another. A serpent for a chemical compound (Kekulé's benzene molecule). The sound of a breaking branch for love.

The Passenger is a narrative that implodes. Its plot is almost impossible to follow; the storyline disperses so that only the essential fragments may emerge.

At the culmination of this process of abandoning narrative form stands *Stella Maris*. Here, McCarthy abolishes entirely the spatial and temporal dimension of storytelling – the backbone of every novel. In place of an ordinary weave of characters and events is the transcription of the dialogues between Alicia and her therapist, Dr. Cohen.

Through these conversations, McCarthy questions Alicia in order to push understanding as far as possible. Some have compared the work to the Platonic dialogues, as though the author wished to dispense with literary invention in order to reach an absolute and abstract contemplation of things (Paolin 2023). Yet what emerges most forcefully – and is purely literary in nature – is the sense of shared humanity exchanged between the two interlocutors, and the warmth Alicia shows in her relationships with the other patients.

Alicia is not shut away within herself. She feels her own humanity beyond the intelligence of numbers and desires the closeness of others:

> I did want to be included. I just wasn't willing to pay the entry fee. On my better days I could even grant that we were the same creatures. Much was the same and little different. The same unlikely forms. Elbows. Skulls. The remnants of a soul. (*Stella Maris* 175)

The importance of affectivity is further underscored by the inclination of both Alicia and Bobby toward music and poetry – the former, an expression without mediation; the latter, the form of verbal language that comes closest to the original through its enigmatic nature and sound. This remains consistent with the recurring emphasis on corporeality against the disembodiment of the world that McCarthy impresses upon the Western siblings.

On this front, the highest point is Alicia's synesthetic capacity, described in several places across the two novels. As we have seen her affirm, she feels numbers – she senses their taste, color, and smell. The same occurs with poetry, to which she has long devoted herself, but especially with music:

> I was musical first. I had perfect pitch. Have. Later I suppose I came to see the world as pretty much proof against any comprehensive description of it. But music seemed to always stand as an exception to everything. It seemed sacrosanct. Autonomous. Completely self-referential and coherent in every part. [...] I was deeply synesthetic and I thought that if music had an inherent reality – color and taste – that only a few people could identify, then perhaps it had other attributes yet to be discerned. The fact that these things were subjective in no way marked them as imaginary. [...]
> *So where does music come from?*
> No one knows. A platonic theory of music just muddies the water. Music is made out of nothing but some fairly simple rules. Yet it's true that no one made them up. The rules. The notes themselves amount to almost nothing. But why some particular arrangement of these notes should have such a profound effect on our emotions is a mystery beyond even the hope of comprehension. Music is not a language. It has no reference to anything other than itself. (*Stella Maris* 38–39)

Alicia places her trust in music just as she does in mathematics. Like mathematics, music exists beyond language.

And she plays the violin, becoming from a very young age an indispensable authority in the authentication of ancient Cremonese violins – in other words, the foremost expert at recognizing that distinctively human capacity to "make through art," transforming something inert like wood into the conduit for a voice that emerges from elsewhere. As is the case with her priceless Amati.

5 On the Edge of the World

> If one wishes to hear an era speak, one must listen to the voices in the rooms where mental distress is treated. If everything inside revolves around the concept of care, something else turns in the opposite direction: the patients' speech. At times they express themselves through unimaginable linguistic con-

> structions – monstrosities (*monstrum*: prodigy) capable of brushing against what we call truth. (Lagioia 2023b, para. 3)

> What if the purpose of human charity wasn't to protect the weak […] but to preserve the mad? Don't they get special treatment in most primitive societies?
> […]
> You have to be careful about who you do away with. (*The Passenger* 329)

The fiction of the world – the farce that involves everyone – can be glimpsed only from the margins, and by those who inhabit these borders. This is true of the mathematicians Alicia describes, above all her principal interlocutor, Grothendieck.

Foucault – never cited, perhaps an unconscious reference – comes here to the fore.

The marginal place *par excellence* is Stella Maris, the psychiatric hospital where Alicia chooses to remain. It is a place where no one but she perceives the prodigy of certain minds that, by subverting the rational order of language, manage to touch something beyond the wall. It is also a place in which care is central – not only in relation to mental illness, as one might ordinarily assume. Alicia takes care of her friends, and they take care of her:

> I think what most people think. That it's caring that heals, not theory. Good the world over. (*Stella Maris* 53)

Even if a poorly contained horror dwells beneath the surface of the world and will never disappear (*Stella Maris* 155), a scattered good nonetheless persists – and Alicia sees it.

The fact remains that she does not choose life.

The one who will manage to live a human life is her brother. He is the one who survives horror, who loves, who suffers, who learns to listen to silence.

That said, Bobby Western is also an exile among exiles. His, too, is a context of relationships in which good appears as closeness, solidarity – as a shared condition among exposed human beings. All his friends – an alcoholic living in a shack (Borman), a dandy in trouble with the law (Sheddan), a transgender woman (Debussy) – embody the wisdom of the dispossessed. They know, as Sheddan reminds Bobby, that it is the collective nature of suffering that makes us human:

> It must surely be true that there is no such collective domain of joy as there is of sorrow. You can't be sure that another man's happiness resembles your own. But where the collective of pain is concerned there can be little doubt at all. If we are not after the essence, Squire, then what are we after? And I'll defer to your view that we cannot uncover such a thing without putting our stamp upon it. And I'll even grant you that you may have drawn the darker cards. But listen to me, Squire. Where the substance of a thing is an uncertain business the form can hardly command more ground. All reality is loss and all loss is eternal. There is no other kind. And that reality into which we inquire must first contain ourselves. (*The Passenger* 378)

There is no refuge in a world shaped by psychological repression. And if, as McCarthy seems to suggest, attempting to understand essence is the destiny of human beings, this does not imply an obsession with hubristic knowledge. It is rather an opening toward the coming of sense – a sentimental leaning toward a beyond, an other. And such a disposition inevitably provokes pain. For this reason, suffering must be lived and passed through, because the reality we seek is still loss: it is the limit within which we move.

The creature at the margins *par excellence* is Debussy, the transgender friend to whom Bobby is most closely attached. And this is no coincidence. Debussy safeguards all the dimensions of human affectivity that allow life to go on, despite everything.

"You're looking at a woman of destiny" (*The Passenger* 63).

Like Alicia, Debussy is stretched toward a relationship with the beyond – in her case, God – which she entrusts to dreaming. What distinguishes her, however, is that she consciously lives and accepts human life for what it is, within the limits afforded her. Life as "nocturnal murmur": like the music of blue notes – rarefied, melancholic, dissonant – inscribed already in her name.

For the first time, McCarthy places female figures at the center of his work. The impression is that the feminine serves as a passage toward origin. Alicia herself possesses an intelligence closer to the original than to the conventional. An exceptional mathematician and musician, she recognizes the worth of other women like herself who have been discriminated against in male-dominated culture (*Stella Maris* 68), highlighting how mechanisms of inferiorization reach deep into history, and how female intelligence has often been equated with madness:

> Women enjoy a different history of madness. From witchcraft to hysteria we're just bad news. We know that women were condemned as witches because they were mentally unstable but no one has considered the numbers – even few as

> they might be – of women who were stoned to death for being bright. That I haven't wound up chained to a cellar wall or burned at the stake is not a testament to our ascending civility but to our ascending skepticism. If we still believed in witches, we'd still be burning them. [...] I'm happy to be treated well but I know that it's an uncertain business. (*Stella Maris* 139)

Yet the one who grasps the feminine in its essence is Debussy – more than any "woman born a woman," conventionally fixed in her gender. She does so precisely because she is a man who wants to be a woman, a man so strained toward origin that she wishes to place herself in a state of transition involving every cell of her being:

> I want to be a woman. I was always envious of girls. Just a little bitch. That's pretty much gone. I know that to be female is an older thing even than to be human. I want to be as old as I can be. Atavistically feminine. (*The Passenger* 65)

> I've been reading about the sexual dimorphism in the brain. It may be more adaptable than people think. It may be that you can change it. You know where this is going because we talked about it. I want to have a female soul. I want the female soul to contain me. That's what I want and that's all I want. [...] That's what I pray for when I pray. To be let in the door. To be a member of the feminine. It doesn't really have anything to do with sex. With having sex. And all the rest is just fluff. (*The Passenger* 70)

Debussy moves toward the original by surpassing Dionysus. She wants to be a woman – not male and female together. In this tension, one glimpses Athena, guardian of the city and the woods, goddess of the tribunal and of war, mediator and huntress – one who synthesizes reason and affection, tends to otherness, and oversees rites of passage and transformation. (Vernant 1985)

For McCarthy, the origin that calls is *Stella Maris* – symbol of the Virgin Mary and of the North Star, metaphor of birth, maternal care, and the course to follow, traced in the night at sea – a summons to the lost art of navigation to be recovered.

In *The Passenger*, Debussy and Bobby take care of one another. To his transgender friend, Bobby entrusts the reading of Alicia's final letter, which he cannot face alone, along with the safeguarding of the others, which are his most precious possessions.

The relationship is steeped in recognition and tenderness. For Debussy, love is the very condition of existence and leads one to choose life, even when, like hers, it is filled with pain. The difference between her and Bobby is that she knows this. Women, McCarthy seems to say, always know more.

Alicia chooses to step away from this edge of the world. Once the farce has been unveiled and the impossibility of beginning again understood – because Bobby is captive to a taboo generated by a reason that prevents him from going as far as she would – accompanied by the recurring dream of a train the two siblings cannot board, she sees no possibility other than to renounce herself.

She does not speak of death, but of the problem of reaching the reality she most desires without being herself. She imagines going to Romania, the land of her ancestors, and, after stripping herself of everything, setting out into the mountains:

> You could have a small fire at night. Maybe find a cave. A mountain stream. I'd have a canteen for water for when the time came that I was too weak to move about. After a while the water would taste extraordinary. It would taste like music. I'd wrap myself in the blanket at night against the cold and watch the bones take shape beneath my skin and I would pray that I might see the truth of the world before I died. Sometimes at night the animals would come to the edge of the fire [...] and I would understand that when the last fire was ashes they would come and carry me away and I would be their eucharist. And that would be my life. And I would be happy. (*Stella Maris* 192)

As Alicia reaches the end, her therapist holds her hand. *Stella Maris* closes on this final gesture, which mirrors and completes the opening of *The Passenger*, where the young woman's body is first discovered.

6 The Sacred

Alicia will never go to Romania. She will not wander through the woods until her body becomes an offering for wild animals. She will not manage to penetrate the sacred – the mystery, the horrific, reality – beyond what her mathematical and synesthetic intelligence allows. She is found by a hunter in the dim winter light of a snowy landscape, on Christmas Day, hanging from a tree.

The one who strips himself of everything is her brother. Bobby's flight is a kind of initiation.

The first stage ends in a shack lost among the dunes of a bay, where he withdraws to live alone, on the edge of survival. He spends his days reading ancient poetry and trying to write letters to Alicia, dead for several years now. It is here that his awareness begins to awaken.

> On sunny days he'd walk the beach naked. Solitary, silent. Lost. Nights he built fires on the beach and sat there wrapped in his blanket. The moon rose over the gulf and the moon's path dished and tilted on the water. Birds flew down the beach in the dark. He didn't know what kind they were. He thought about the passenger but he never went back out to the islands. The fire leaned in the wind and seawater hissed in the burning wood. [...]
>
> He knew that he should wonder what was to become of him. (*The Passenger* 272)

At this point, the Thalidomide Kid appears.

> *We go back a bit. One way or another. Me and thee.*
> By hearsay. How do I know what to trust?
> *You don't have a choice. All you can believe is what is. Unless you'd prefer to believe what ain't. I'd have thought we might be past all that by now.* (*The Passenger* 273)

The Kid invites him to ask questions, but Bobby does not trust him. Repeatedly provoked, he finally decides to speak, trying to understand what sort of creature he is encountering.

Did the Thalidomide Kid really know about Alicia? How had he found him? Where would he go afterward?

As they walk along the beach – "out at sea the ragged wire filaments of lightning stood briefly and then again along the darkening rim of the world" – the Kid tells him that he was a rib of Alicia's psyche and perhaps now of his as well. "It's just a plague of fucking mysteries aint it?" Bobby is not the only one clinging to a wreck; when the Kid is finished with him, he will go "elsewhere" (*The Passenger* 273–274).

Irritated, he adds that he did not come to talk about the weather. At yet another provocation, Western gives in and asks what would have happened if the Kid and his "little friends" had left Alicia alone. "Hey. A question," the Kid replies. He believes he extended her life – though he does not know who that "evil little shit from some heretofore unknown hinterworld" was, who wanted to "gear up for the big one" by penetrating the organizational structure (*ibid.*, 277).

And yet he admits he never understood whether he truly helped her:

> *The world's a deceptive place. A lot of things that you see are not really there anymore. Just the after-image in the eye. So to speak.*
> What did she know?
> *She knew that in the end you really cant know. You cant get hold of the world. You can only draw a picture. Whether it's a bull on the wall of a cave or a partial differential equation it's all the same thing.* (*The Passenger* 279)

Alicia was different. "She wouldn't profile" (*ibid.*, 280). She didn't fit any template. Bobby asks whether the template is an electronic model capable of mapping mental terrain, but receives no answer. For the Kid, his sister was simply an anomaly – a bug in the system – unlike Bobby, whom he finds so obtuse that he is forced into a harsh, direct, almost cruel register:

> *Anyway, you don't really want to talk. You just want somebody to tell you that it's not your fault.*
> [...]
> *your problem is that you don't really believe that she's dead.*
> [...]
> *Anyway, you still got yourself to go.*
> [...]
> *Who knows?* said the Kid. *Maybe you and Sis can rendezvous in the sweet by-and-by.* (*The Passenger* 281–282)

At this, Bobby finally breaks open in all his grief.

The Kid disappears.

The next morning, Robert Western slowly comes back to himself, speaking with Alicia until he feels her touch on his cheek:

> You don't know what you're asking.
> *Fateful words.*
> She touched his cheek. *I don't have to.*
> You don't know how it will end.
> *I don't care how it will end. I only care about now.* (*The Passenger* 283)

It no longer matters what is real and what is not. Bobby decides to face suffering. He will live as a hermit in Idaho. He will speak to her, write to her, knowing that sooner or later everything will begin to fade. He returns to Stella Maris to speak with those who knew her, then returns to Knoxville to say goodbye to his old friends, leaving the city for good.

In the final chapter, we find him on a Spanish island, living in an old mill belonging to a friend. Even there, he is visited by Alicia and by Sheddan – also dead – who, reminding him that passing through suffering is not the same as condemning oneself to unhappiness, leaves him with a final piece of advice:

> To prepare for any struggle is largely a work of unburdening oneself. If you carry your past into battle you are riding to your death. Austerity lifts the heart and focuses the vision. Travel light. A few ideas are enough. (*The Passenger* 379)

A few ideas, a little logic – some grammar; a few physics books; but above all poetry and silence – so that suffering may be faced, loss accepted, and life lived without guilt, for what it is. This is the challenge.

Bobby becomes his existence:

> the last pagan on earth, singing softly upon his pallet in an unknown tongue. (*The Passenger* 383)

Bibliography

Adkins, Arthur W.H. 1972. *Moral Values and Political Behaviour in Ancient Greece: From Homer to the End of the Fifth Century*. London: Chatto & Windus.

Aeschylus. *Eumenides*. 1926. Translated by Herbert Weir Smyth. Loeb Classical Library. Cambridge: Harvard University Press.

Anaximander. *Fragments*. 1962. In William K.C. Guthrie, *A History of Greek Philosophy*, Vol. 1. *The Earlier Presocratics and the Pythagoreans*. Cambridge: Cambridge University Press.

Andreotti, Angelo. 2018. *Il nascosto dell'opera. Frammenti sull'eticità dell'arte*. Ancona: Italic.

Antaki, Mark. 2019. "Le tournant sensoriel en droit: Vers un droit sensible et sensé?" *Canadian Journal of Law and Society / Revue canadienne Droit et Société* 34(2): 361–370.

Avitabile, Luisa. 2004. *La filosofia del diritto in Pierre Legendre*. Turin: Giappichelli.

Avitabile, Luisa, ed. 2011. *Il diritto tra forma e formalismo*. Naples: Editoriale Scientifica.

Bachmann, Ingeborg. 2006. "Bohemia Lies by the Sea". In *Darkness Spoken: The Collected Poems of Ingeborg Bachmann*. Translated by Peter Filkins. Tucson: Zephyr Press.

Bandes, Susan A., ed. 1999. *The Passions of Law*. New York: New York University Press.

Bently, Lionel, and Leo Flynn, eds. 1996. *Law and the Senses: Sensational Jurisprudence*. London: Pluto Press.

Bodei, Remo. 2016. *Limite*. Bologna: Il Mulino.

Bodei, Remo, *et al.* 2017. *Le virtù cardinali*. Rome–Bari: Laterza.

Bollas, Christopher. 2018. *Meaning and Melancholia. Life in the Age of Bewilderment*. Oxon and New York: Routledge.

Borutti, Silvana. 2006. *Filosofia dei sensi. Estetica del pensiero tra filosofia, arte e letteratura*. Milan: Cortina.

Branco, Patrícia, and Valerio Nitrato Izzo. 2017. "Intersections in Law, Culture and the Humanities." *Revista Crítica de Ciências Sociais* 112: 45–72.

Brunello, Mario. 2014. *Silenzio*. Bologna: Il Mulino.

Cage, John. 2015. *Silence*. London: Boyars.

Calabresi, Guido. 1989. "Introductory Letter." *Yale Journal of Law & the Humanities* 1 (1): vii–viii.

Campanale, Anna Maria. 2016. *Nomos e eikon. Immagini dell'esperienza giuridica*. Turin: Giappichelli.

Cananzi, Daniele. 2013. *Formatività e norma. Elementi di teoria estetica dell'interpretazione giuridica*. Turin: Giappichelli.

Cananzi, Daniele. 2016. *Percorsi ermeneutici di filosofia del diritto. Lezioni*, Vol. 2. Turin: Giappichelli.

Cananzi, Daniele. 2017a. *Estetica del diritto. Sul fondamento geologico del giuridico. Lezioni*, Vol. 3. Turin: Giappichelli.

Cananzi, Daniele. 2017b. "Introduzione." In Carnelutti 2017, xvii–xviii.

Capograssi, Giuseppe. 1959. *L'attualità di Vico*. In *Opere*, Vol. 4, 395–410. Milan: Giuffrè.

Capograssi, Giuseppe. 1962. *Il problema della scienza del diritto*. Milan: Giuffrè.

Carnelutti, Francesco. 2017. *Arte del diritto*. Turin: Giappichelli.

Casonato, Carlo. 2020. "Intelligenza artificiale e giustizia: potenzialità e rischi." *DPCE Online* 44(3). Intelligenza artificiale e giustizia: potenzialità e rischi: Artificial Intelligence and Justice: Potentialities and Risks | DPCE Online [accessed 24 Jan. 2026].

Cassano, Franco. 1989. *Approssimazione. Esercizi di esperienza dell'altro*. Bologna: Il Mulino.

Casucci, Felice, ed. 2013. *Il silenzio del diritto*. Naples: ESI.

Cioran, Emil M. 1968. *The Temptation to Exist*. Translated by Richard Howard. Chicago: Quadrangle Books.

Colli, Giorgio. 2006. *La sapienza greca,*Vol. II. *Epimenide – Ferecide – Talete – Anassimandro – Anassimene – Onomacrito*. Milan: Adelphi.

Cometa, Michele. 2020. "Verso una topica dell'immaginazione. Lo iato e la nascita delle immagini." In Laura Follesa, ed., *Il 'pensiero per immagini' e le forme dell'invisibile / Das 'Denken in Bildern' und die Formen des Unsichtbaren*, 235–251. Berlin: Peter Lang.

Condello, Angela, and Paolo Heritier, eds. 2021. "The Myth of the Law through the Mirror of Humanities: Perspectives on Law, Literature, Psychoanalysis, and Aesthetics." Special issue, *Law and Literature* 33(2).

Constable, Marianne. 2005. *Just Silences: The Limits and Possibilities of Modern Law*. Princeton: Princeton University Press.

Cotta, Sergio. 1978. *Perché la violenza? Un'interpretazione filosofica*. L'Aquila: Japadre.

Crespi, Franco. 1994. *Imparare ad esistere. Nuovi fondamenti della solidarietà sociale*. Rome: Donzelli.

Curi, Umberto. 2013. *Passione*. Milan: Cortina.

D'Agostino, Francesco. 1979. *Per un'archeologia del diritto. Miti giuridici greci*. Milan: Giuffrè.

D'Arzo, Silvio. 2002. *Casa d'altri*. Edited by Paolo Briganti and Andrea Briganti. Parma: Diabasis.

Dalmasso, Gianfranco. 2012. "Il pudore come fattore politico." *Spazio Filosofico* 5: 181–185.

De Blasio, Antonella. 2011. *Sulla sinestesia. Passato e futuro*. Bologna: Archetipo.

Derrida, Jacques. 1991. *Donner le temps*, Vol. 1. *La fausse monnaie*. Paris: Éditions Galilée.

Douzinas, Costas, and Lynda Nead, eds. 1999. *Law and the Image: The Authority of Art, The Aesthetics of Law*. Chicago: University of Chicago Press.

Dufourmantelle Anne. 2024. *L'intelligence du rêve. Fantasmes, apparitions, inspiration*. Paris: Payot & Rivages.

Eco, Umberto. 2001. *Apocalittici e integrati*. Milan: Bompiani.

Esposito, Roberto. 2015. *Persons and Things*. Translated by Zakiya Hanafi. Cambridge: Polity Press.

Faralli, Carla. 2022. *Le grandi correnti della filosofia del diritto*. Turin: Giappichelli.

Ferrari, Vincenzo. 2020. "Note socio-giuridiche introduttive per una discussione su diritto, intelligenza artificiale e big data." *Sociologia del diritto* 47(3): 9–32.

Forza, Antonio, Giulia Menegon, and Rino Rumiati. 2017. *Il giudice emotivo. La decisione tra ragione ed emozione*. Bologna: Il Mulino.

Franca-Filho, Marcilio T. 2014. "Multisensory Law and Italo Calvino's *Lezioni Americane*." *Comparative Law Review* 5: 1–20.

Galgano, Francesco. 2010. *Le insidie del linguaggio giuridico. Saggio sulle metafore nel diritto*. Bologna: Il Mulino.

Galimberti, Umberto. 1999. *Psiche e techne. L'uomo nell'età della tecnica*. Milan: Feltrinelli.

Garapon, Antoine, and Jean Lassègue. 2018. *Justice digitale: révolution graphique et rupture anthropologique*. Paris: Presses universitaires de France (PUF).

Gehlen, Arnold. 1988. *Man: His Nature and Place in the World*. Translated by Clare McMillan and Karl Pillemer. New York: Columbia University Press.

Gernet, Louis. 1917. *Recherches sur le développement de la pensée juridique et morale en Grèce. Étude sémantique*. Paris: Leroux.

Gilli, Gian Antonio. 1988. *Origini dell'eguaglianza. Ricerche sociologiche sull'antica Grecia*. Turin: Einaudi.

Givone, Sergio. 2003. *Prima lezione di estetica*. Rome–Bari: Laterza.

Grabham, Emily. 2009. "Shaking Mr. Jones: Law and Touch." *International Journal of Law in Context* 5(4): 343–353.

Greco, Tommaso. 2005. "Dal dolore alla giustizia. Strategie di risposta tra carità e diritto." In Vincenzo Omaggio, ed., *Diritto in trasformazione*, 407–440. Naples: Editoriale Scientifica.

Greco, Tommaso. 2009. "Senza benda né spada. L'immagine weiliana della giustizia." In Stefania Tarantino, ed., *Pensiero e giustizia in Simone Weil*, 111–132. Rome: Aracne.

Greco, Tommaso. 2012. "Il ritorno dei doveri." *Cultura e Diritti. Per una formazione giuridica* 1(1): 91–98.

Guthrie, William K.C. 1962. *A History of Greek Philosophy*, Vol. 1. *The Earlier Presocratics and the Pythagoreans*. Cambridge: Cambridge University Press.

Guardini, Romano. 1980. *Virtù*. Brescia: Morcelliana.

Hamilton, Sheryl N., *et al.*, 2017. *Sensing Law*. London and New York: Routledge.

Han, Byung-Chul. 2017a. *The Scent of Time: A Philosophical Essay on the Art of Lingering*. Translated by Daniel Steuer. Cambridge: Polity Press.

Han, Byung-Chul. 2017b. *Shanzhai: Deconstruction in Chinese*. Translated by Philippa Hurd. Cambridge, MA: MIT Press.

Han, Byung-Chul. 2021. *The Palliative Society. Pain Today*. Translated by Daniel Steuer. Cambridge and Medford: Polity Press.

Heidegger, Martin. 2002. *Off the Beaten Track*. Edited and translated by Julian Young and Kenneth Haynes. Cambridge: Cambridge University Press.

Heritier, Paolo. 2012. *Estetica giuridica*. Vol. 1, *Primi elementi. Dalla globalizzazione alla secolarizzazione*; Vol. 2, *A partire da Legendre. Il fondamento finzionale del diritto positivo*. Turin: Giappichelli.

Heritier, Paolo. 2013. "Law and Image: Towards a Theory in Nomograms." In Richard K. Sherwin and Anne Wagner, eds., *Law, Culture and Visual Studies*, 24–48. Dordrecht–Heidelberg–New York–London: Springer.

Heritier, Paolo. 2016. "Giustizia affettiva, metodo retorico, neuroscienze. Un itinerario tra Aristotele e Vico a partire da Alessandro Giuliani." In Pierangelo Siqueri, *Deontologia del fondamento*, 91–134. Turin: Giappichelli.

Hesiod. *Theogony*. 1914. In *The Homeric Hymns and Homerica*. Translated by H.G. Evelyn-White. Loeb Classical Library. London: William Heinemann; New York: The Macmillan Co.

Hesiod. *Works and Days*. 1914. In *The Homeric Hymns and Homerica*. Translated by H.G. Evelyn-White. Loeb Classical Library. London: William Heinemann; New York: The Macmillan Co.

Hibbitts, Bernard J. 1992. "Coming to Our Senses: Communication and Legal Expression in Performance Cultures." *Emory Law Journal* 41: 873–960.

Homer. *Odyssey*. 1919–1920. Translated by A. T. Murray. Loeb Classical Library. Cambridge: Harvard University Press. (Revised edition by George E. Dimock, 1995).

Howes, David. 2013. "The Expanding Field of Sensory Studies v. 1.0." *Sensory Studies*. http://www.sensorystudies.org/sensorial-investigations/the-expanding-field-of-sensory-studies/ [Accessed 23 Jan. 2026].

Howes, David, ed. 2019. "Troubling Law's Sensorium: Explorations in Sensational Jurisprudence." Special Issue, *Canadian Journal of Law and Society* 34(2).

Hugo, Victor. 2000. *Les Misérables*. Translated by Charles E. Wilbour. New York: Modern Library.

Irti, Natalino. 2007. *Il salvagente della forma*. Rome–Bari: Laterza.

Jabès, Edmond. 1989. *The Book of Shares*. Translated by Rosmarie Waldrop. Chicago: University of Chicago Press.

Jabès, Edmond. 1991. *Le Livre de l'Hospitalité*. Paris: Gallimard.

Jaeger, Werner. 1944. *Paideia: The Ideals of Greek Culture*, Vol. 3. *The Conflict of Cultural Ideals in the Age of Plato*. Translated by: Gilbert Highet. New York and London: Oxford University Press.

Jauss, Hans-Robert. 1982. "Aesthetic Pleasure and the Fundamental Experiences of Poiesis, Aesthesis, and Catharsis." In *Aesthetic Experience and Literary Hermeneutics*, 22–36. Translated by Michael Shaw. Minneapolis: University of Minnesota Press.

Jedlowski, Paolo. 2008. *Il sapere dell'esperienza. Fra l'abitudine e il dubbio*. Rome: Carocci.

Jonas, Hans. 1984. *The Imperative of Responsibility. In Search of an Ethics for the Technological Age*. Translated by Hans Jonas with the collaboration of David Herr. Chicago: The University of Chicago Press.

Jullien, François. 2013. *De l'intime: loin du bruyant Amour*. Paris: Grasset.

Jullien, François. 2018a. *Alterità. Lezioni milanesi per la Cattedra Rotelli*, edited by Caterina Piccione. Milan and Udine: Mimesis.

Jullien, François. 2018b. *De-coincidence: Where Art and Existence Come From*. Translated by Pedro Rodríguez. Taipei: National Taiwan University of Arts.

Jullien, François. 2020. *De la vraie vie*. Paris: Éditions de l'Observatoire.

Jullien, François. 2025. *Puissance du pensif: ou comment pense la littérature*. Arles: Actes Sud.

Kafka, Franz. 1919. *In the Penal Colony*. Translated by Ian Johnston. Vancouver Island University web text. https://web.viu.ca/johnstoi/kafka/inthepenalcolony.htm [Accessed 23 Jan. 2026].

Kim, Ki-Duk. 2012. *Pietà*. South Korea, 104 min.

Kiefer, Anselm. 2011. *L'art survivra à ses ruines. Anselm Kiefer au Collège de France (2010–2011)*. Paris: Éditions du Regard.

Kapoor, Anish. 2015. "Anish Kapoor Presents *Descension*, Galleria Continua, San Gimignano." YouTube video. https://www.youtube.com/watch?v=x7sxozsUjP4 . [accessed 24 Jan. 2026].

Lagioia, Nicola. 2023a. "*Il passeggero* di Cormac McCarthy è destinato a restare, a differenza di noi." *Lucy sulla cultura*, 16 May. https://lucysullacultura.com/il-passeggero-di-cormac-mccarthy-e-un-romanzo-destinato-a-restare-a-differenza-di-noi [accessed 24 Jan. 2026].

Lagioia, Nicola. 2023b. "Alle domande si arriva col linguaggio, alle risposte con l'inconscio: *Stella Maris* di Cormac McCarthy." *Lucy sulla cultura*, 19 October. https://lucysullacultura.com/alle-domande-si-arriva-col-linguaggio-alle-risposte-con-linconscio-stella-maris-di-cormac-mccarthy/ [accessed 24 Jan. 2026].

LeBaron, Michelle. 2020. "The Deepest Sense: Revitalizing Links Between Law and Touch." In Danilo Mandic, *et al.*, eds. *TOUCH*. London: Non Liquet, The Westminster Online Working Papers Series, 67–85. https://www.westminster.ac.uk/sites/default/public-files/general-documents/Touch.pdf [accessed 24 Jan. 2026].

Lewis, John D. 2006. *Solon the Thinker: Political Thought in Archaic Athens*. London and New York: Bloomsbury Academic Publishing.

Limone, Giuseppe. 2004. "Fra Grozio e Vico: il problema del 'diritto naturale' come teoresi rigorosa." In Vanda Fiorillo and Friedrich Vollhardt, eds., *Il diritto naturale della socialità. Tradizioni antiche e antropologia moderna nel XVII secolo*, 51–77. Turin: Giappichelli.

Limone, Giuseppe. 2019. "Il pudore, la responsabilità. Il *Protagora* di Platone interroga i tempi contemporanei?" In "Il pudore delle cose, la responsabilità delle azioni," 7–74. *L'era di Antigone – Quaderno n. 11*. Milan: Angeli.

Maldiney, Henry. 2013. "L'esthétique des rythmes" (1967). In *Regard Parole Espace*, 201–230. Paris: Les Éditions du Cerf.

Manacorda, Giorgio. 2016. *La poesia*. Rome: Castelvecchi.

Mandic, Danilo, *et al.*, eds. 2015. *SMELL*. London: University of Westminster Press. https://nonliquetlaw.files.wordpress.com/2015/04/law-and-the-senses_smell.pdf [accessed 24 Jan. 2026].

Marcantonio, Erika. 2012. "Comunità e coesistenza." In Ugo Perone, ed., *Intorno a Jean-Luc Nancy*, 23–27. Turin: Rosenberg & Sellier.

Marusek, Sarah, ed. 2020. *Synesthetic Legalities: Sensory Dimensions of Law and Jurisprudence*. London and New York: Routledge.

Masciandaro, Nicola. 2018. "Synaesthesia. The Mystical Sense of Law." In Andreas Philippopoulos-Mihalopoulos, ed., *Routledge Research Handbook on Law and Theory*, 179–201. London and New York: Routledge.

Massaro, Tony. 1989. "Empathy, Legal Storytelling, and the Rule of Law: New Words, Old Wounds." *Michigan Law Review* 87 (8): 2099–2127.

Masullo, Aldo. 2003. *Paticità e indifferenza*. Genoa: Il Melangolo.

Mati, Susanna. 2010. *La decisione di Platone. Sulla 'condanna dell'arte'*. Genoa: Il Melangolo.

McCarthy, Cormac. 2017. "The Kekulé Problem. Where Did Language Come From," *Nautilus* 17 April. https://nautil.us/the-kekul-problem-236574/ [accessed 24 Jan. 2026].

McCarthy, Cormac. 2022. *The Passenger*. New York: Penguin.

McCarthy, Cormac. 2022. *Stella Maris*. New York: Penguin.

Messner, Claudius. 2018. "Now This: On the Gradual Production of Justice Whilst Doing Law and Music." *International Journal for the Semiotics of Law* 31: 187–214.

Mittica, M. Paola. 2006. *Raccontando il possibile. Eschilo e le narrazioni giuridiche*. Milan: Giuffrè.

Mittica, M. Paola. 2007. *Cantori di nostoi. Strutture giuridiche e politiche delle comunità omeriche*. Rome: Aracne.

Mittica, M. Paola. 2012. "Attraversare il silenzio. I presupposti impliciti del diritto." *Sociologia del diritto* 2: 55–76.

Mittica, M. Paola. 2015. "When the world was mousiké: on the origins of the relationship between law and music." *Law and Humanities* 9(1): 29–54.

Mittica, M. Paola. 2017. "Ritmo e trasformazione. Sulla via dell'estetica giuridica." *Materiali per una storia della cultura giuridica* 47(1): 67–85.

Mittica, M. Paola. 2021. "In quest of sense. The way towards an Aesthetics of Law through Law and Humanities." *Law & Literature* 33(2): 171–188.

Mittica, M. Paola. 2023. "Narration as a threshold in the search for meaning." *Undecidabilities and Law* 3: 45–55.

Moravia, Sergio. 1995. "Esistenza e passione." In Silvia Vegetti Finzi, ed., *Storia delle passioni*, 3–38. Rome–Bari: Laterza.

Musil, Robert. 1995. *The Man Without Qualities.* Translated by Sophie Wilkins. London: Picador.

Nancy, Jean-Luc. 1996. *The Muses.* Translated by Peggy Kamuf. Stanford: Stanford University Press.

Nancy, Jean-Luc. 1997a. *The Sense of the World.* Translated by Jeffrey S. Librett. Minneapolis: University of Minnesota Press.

Nancy, Jean-Luc. 1997b. *Résistance de la poésie.* Bordeaux: William Blake & Co / Art & Arts.

Nancy, Jean-Luc. 2003. *A Finite Thinking.* Translated by Steven Miller *et al.* Stanford: Stanford University Press.

Nancy, Jean-Luc. 2004. *58 indices sur le corps.* Montréal: Nota Bene Editions.

Nancy, Jean-Luc. 2008a. *Corpus.* Translated by Richard A. Rand. New York: Fordham University Press.

Nancy, Jean-Luc. 2008b. *Le poids d'une pensée, l'approche.* Paris: Edition de la Phocide.

Natoli, Salvatore. 2002. *Stare al mondo. Escursioni nel tempo presente.* Milan: Feltrinelli.

Natoli, Salvatore. 2008a. *L'esperienza del dolore. Le forme del patire nella cultura occidentale.* Milan: Feltrinelli.

Natoli, Salvatore. 2008b. *Dizionario dei vizi e delle virtù.* Milan: Feltrinelli.

Natoli, Salvatore. 2010a. *Il buon uso del mondo.* Milan: Mondadori.

Natoli, Salvatore. 2010b. *L'edificazione di sé. Istruzioni sulla vita interiore.* Rome–Bari: Laterza.

Natoli, Salvatore. 2016. *Il rischio di fidarsi.* Bologna: Il Mulino.

Nifosì, Giuseppe. 2020. "L'Annunciazione del Beato Angelico." *Arte svelata – Blog.* https://www.artesvelata.it [accessed 24 Jan. 2026].

Nirta, Caterina, *et al.*, eds. 2020. *TOUCH.* London: University of Westminster Press. https://doi.org/10.16997/book37 [accessed 24 Jan. 2026].

Nitrato Izzo, Valerio. 2017. *Gli spazi giuridici della città contemporanea. Rappresentazioni e pratiche.* Naples: Editoriale Scientifica.

Nucci, Matteo. 2013. *Le lacrime degli eroi*. Turin: Einaudi.

Orazi, Massimiliano. 2020. *Del pudore. Per una filosofia dell'alterità e della misura*. Turin: Giappichelli.

Ost, François. 1999. *Le temps du droit*. Paris: Jacob.

Ost, François. 2018. *Le droit, objet de passions? I crave the law*. Brussels: Académie royale de Belgique.

Ost, François. 2021. *Le droit ou l'empire du tiers*. Paris: Dalloz.

Paolin, Demetrio. 2023. "*Stella Maris*: il linguaggio, il fuoco e l'eucarestia di sé." *La ricerca*, 31 October. https://laricerca.loescher.it/stella-maris-il-linguaggio-il-fuoco-e-leucarestia-di-se/ [accessed 24 Jan. 2026].

Pareyson, Luigi. 1954. *Estetica. Teoria della formatività*. Milan: Feltrinelli.

Pavoni, Andrea, *et al.*, eds. 2018a. *TASTE*. London: University of Westminster Press. https://doi.org/10.16997/book21 [accessed 24 Jan. 2026].

Pavoni, Andrea, *et al.*, eds. 2018b. *SEE*. London: University of Westminster Press. https://doi.org/10.16997/book12 [accessed 24 Jan. 2026].

Pinotti, Andrea. 2011. *Empatia. Storia di un'idea da Platone al post-umano*. Rome–Bari: Laterza.

Philippopoulos-Mihalopoulos, Andreas. 2013. "Atmospheres of Law: Senses, Affects, Lawscapes." *Emotion, Space and Society* 7: 35–44.

Plato. *Protagoras*. 1892. In *The Dialogues of Plato*. Translated by Benjamin Jowett. Oxford: Clarendon Press.

Pons, Alain. 2005. "... Il rossore, di cui certamente niuna fu mai al mondo nazione che non si tinse ..." In Giuseppe Cacciatore *et al.*, eds., *Il corpo e le sue facoltà. G.B. Vico*. Laboratorio dell'ISPF II(1), 277–289. http://www.ispf-lab.cnr.it/content/atti-del-convegno-internazionale-il-corpo-e-le-sue-facoltà-gb-vico-napoli-3-6-novembre-2004- [accessed 24 Jan. 2026].

Prete, Antonio. 2013. *Compassione. Storia di un sentimento*. Turin: Bollati Boringhieri.

Prete, Antonio. 2016. *Il cielo nascosto. Grammatica dell'interiorità*. Turin: Bollati Boringhieri.

Pulcini, Elena. 2009. *La cura del mondo. Paura e responsabilità nell'età globale*. Turin: Bollati Boringhieri.

Pulcini, Elena. 2020. *Tra cura e giustizia. Le passioni come risorsa sociale*. Turin: Bollati Boringhieri.

Rella, Franco. 1987. *Limina. Il pensiero e le cose*. Milan: Feltrinelli.

Remotti, Francesco. 2017. *L'ossessione identitaria*. Rome–Bari: Laterza.

Resta, Eligio. 2009. *Le regole della fiducia*. Rome–Bari: Laterza.

Rigby, Kate. 2007. *Thalidomide Kid*. Langley, BC, Canada: Bewrite Books.

Ricoeur, Paul. 1966. *Philosophy of the Will*, Vol. 1. *Freedom and Nature: The Voluntary and the Involuntary*. Edited by J. Wilde. Chicago: Northwestern University Press.

Rigotti, Francesca. 2021. *L'era del singolo*. Turin: Einaudi.

Rilke, Rainer Maria. 1960. "The Life of Mary." In *Selected Works,* Vol. 2. Translated by James B. Leishman. London: Hogarth Press.

Robilant, Anna di. 2001. "Non soltanto parole. In margine ad alcuni itinerari in Law and Art." *Materiali per una storia della cultura giuridica* 31(2): 483–513.

Romano, Bruno. 2006. *Scienza giuridica senza giurista: il nichilismo giuridico perfetto.* Turin: Giappichelli.

Romano, Bruno. 2012. *Forma del senso. Legalità e giustizia.* Turin: Giappichelli.

Rouland, Norbert. 2005. *Du droit aux passions.* Aix-en-Provence: Presses de l'Université d'Aix-Marseille I.

Rovatti, Pier Aldo. 1992. *L'esercizio del silenzio.* Milan: Cortina.

Rovatti, Pier Aldo. 2007. *Abitare la distanza: per una pratica della filosofia.* Milan: Cortina.

Sappho. *Deathless Aphrodite.* 2002. In *If Not, Winter: Fragments of Sappho.* Translated by Anne Carson. New York: Knopf Doubleday Publishing Group.

Santos, Boaventura de Sousa. 2018. *The End of the Cognitive Empire: The Coming of Age of Epistemologies of the South.* Durham: Duke University Press.

Sapochnik, Miguel. 2021. *Finch.* UK–USA, 118 min.

Sarat, Austin, Matthew Anderson, and Cathrine O. Frank, eds. 2010. *Law and the Humanities. An Introduction.* New York: Cambridge University Press.

Satta, Salvatore. 1994. *Il mistero del processo.* Milan: Adelphi.

Savona, Pier Francesco. 2005. *In limine juris. La genesi extra ordinem della giuridicità e il sentimento del diritto.* Naples: Edizioni Scientifiche Italiane.

Sbriccoli, Mario. 2009. "La benda della giustizia. Iconografia, diritto e leggi penali dal medioevo all'età moderna." In *Storia del diritto penale e della giustizia,* Vol. I. *Scritti editi e inediti (1972–2007),* 155–208. Milan: Giuffrè.

Sellers, Mortimer N. S., ed. 2017. *Law, Reason and Emotion.* Cambridge and New York: Cambridge University Press.

Sterpa, Alessandro. 2021. "Diritti e corpo. Elementi per una riflessione." *Federalismi* 11: 176–201.

Supiot, Alain. 2007. *Homo juridicus: On the Anthropological Function of the Law.* Translated by Saskia Brown. London and New York: Verso Books.

Supiot, Alain. 2020. *La sovranità del limite. Giustizia, lavoro e ambiente nell'orizzonte della mondializzazione.* Edited by Andrea Allamprese and Luca d'Ambrosio. Afterword by Ota De Leonardis. Milan and Udine: Mimesis.

Ventura, Raffaele Alberto. 2020. *Radical choc. Ascesa e caduta dei competenti.* Turin: Einaudi.

Vernant, Jean-Pierre. 1985. *La mort dans les yeux. Figures de l'Autre en Grèce ancienne.* Paris: Hachette littératures.

Vogliotti, Massimo. 2007. *Tra fatto e diritto. Oltre la modernità giuridica.* Turin: Giappichelli.

Walcott, Derek. 2004. *The Prodigal: A Poem* (section 3.II). New York: Farrar, Straus and Giroux.

Weil, Simone. 2024. *The Need for Roots.* Translated by Ros Schwartz. London: Penguin Classics.

West, Robin. 2015. “Law’s Emotions.” *Richmond Journal of Law and the Public Interest* 19: 339–362.

White, James Boyd. 1984. *When Words Lose Their Meaning.* Chicago: University of Chicago Press.

Yourcenar, Marguerite. 1981. *The Abyss.* Translated by Grace Frick. New York: Farrar, Straus and Giroux.

Zanetti, Gianfrancesco. 2011. *Vico eversivo.* Bologna: Il Mulino.

Zeidler, Kamil. 2020. *Aesthetics of Law.* Warsaw: Gdańsk University Press – Wolters Kluwer.

By the Same Author

Monographs

Diritto e letteratura e Law and Humanities. Elementi per un'estetica giuridica (Law and Literature and Law and Humanities: Elements for a legal aesthetics). Turin: Giappichelli, 2024.

Il pensiero che sente. Pratiche di Law and Humanities (The Thinking That Feels: Practices in Law and Humanities). Turin: Giappichelli, 2022.

Cantori di nostoi. Strutture giuridiche e politiche delle comunità omeriche (Singers of Nostoi Juridical and Political Structures in Homeric Communities). Rome: Aracne, 2007.

Raccontando il possibile. Eschilo e le narrazioni giuridiche (Telling the Possible: Aeschylus and Legal Narratives). Milan: Giuffrè, 2006.

Il divenire dell'ordine. L'interazione normativa nella società omerica (The Becoming of Order. Normative Interaction in Homeric Society). Milan: Giuffrè, 1996.

Edited Volumes

Il diritto tra testo e immagine. Rappresentazione ed evoluzione delle fonti (Law between Text and Image. Representation and Evolution of Legal Sources), with C. Faralli, V. Gigliotti, and P. Heritier (eds.). Milan: Mimesis, 2014.

Arte e limite. La misura del diritto (Art and Limit. The Measure of Law), with A. C. Amato Mangiameli and C. Faralli (eds.). Rome: Aracne, 2012.

Diritto e narrazioni. Temi di diritto, letteratura e altre arti (Law and Narratives. Themes in Law, Literature, and the Other Arts). Milan: Ledizioni, 2011.

Diritto e letteratura. Prospettive di ricerca (Law and Literature. Research Perspectives), with C. Faralli (ed.). Rome: Aracne, 2010.

Concetti e norme. Teorie e ricerche di antropologia giuridica (Concepts and Norms. Theories and Research in Legal Anthropology), with A. Facchi (ed.). Milan: FrancoAngeli, 2000.

Selected Articles

"Passavamo sulla terra leggeri: Corologia ed etica del nomadismo" (We Walked Lightly on the Earth: Chorology and Ethics of Nomadism). *Sudeuropa* 1, 2025, 61–72.

HTTPS://DOI.ORG/10.1163/9789004757714-009

"Narration as a Threshold in the Search for Meaning." *Undecidabilities and Law* 3, 2023, 45–55. Available online: https://doi.org/10.14195/2184-9781_3_3

"O sentido do sentir: Law and Humanities e Estética jurídica" (The Sense of Feeling: Law and Humanities and Aesthetics of Law). *Revista da Faculdade de Direito UFPR* 68(3), 2023, 163–180. Available online: http://dx.doi.org/10.5380/rfdufpr.v68i3.94723

"Sur la voie de la sociologie du droit. L'approche de Droit et musique" (On the Path of the Sociology of Law: The Law and Music Approach). *Droit et Société* 107(1), 2021, 105–118. Available online: https://doi.org/10.3917/drs1.107.0105

"Disabitare. Cittadini e città del nostro tempo" (Inhabiting Otherwise: Citizens and Cities of Our Time). *Sudeuropa* 3, 2020, 19–38.

"In Quest of Sense. The Way towards an Aesthetics of Law through Law and Humanities." *Law & Literature* 33(2), 2021, 171–188. Available online: https://doi.org/10.1080/1535685X.2021.1847795

"C'era una volta il diritto. A proposito di *Si le droit m'était conté* di François Ost" (Once Upon a Time There Was Law: On *Si le droit m'était conté* by François Ost). *Sociologia del diritto* 2, 2020, 184–198. Available online: https://doi.org/10.3280/SD2020-002009

"Ritmo e trasformazione. Sulla via dell'estetica giuridica" (Rhythm and Transformation: On the Path toward Aesthetics of Law). *Materiali per una storia della cultura giuridica* 47(1), 2017, 67–85.

"When the World Was Mousiké: On the Origins of the Relationship between Law and Music." *Law and Humanities* 9(1), 2015, 29–54. Available online: https://doi.org/10.1080/17521483.2015.1042219

"The Deception of Cadence: Toward a Dissonant Law." *Law and Humanities* 7(2), 2013, pp. 151–169. Available online: https://doi.org/10.5235/17521483.7.2.151

"Attraversare il silenzio. I presupposti impliciti del diritto" (Crossing Silence: The Implicit Presuppositions of Law). *Sociologia del diritto* 2, 2012, 55–76. Available online: https://doi.org/10.3280/SD2012-002006

"The Heart of Law." *No Foundations* 9, 2012, 97–118.

"Diritto e costruzione narrativa. La connessione tra diritto e letteratura" (Law and Narrative Construction: The Connection between Law and Literature). *Tigor* 1, 2010, 14–23.

"Diritto e letteratura in Italia. Stato dell'arte e riflessione sul metodo" (Law and Literature in Italy: State of the Art and Reflections on Method). *Materiali per una storia della cultura giuridica* 39(1), 2009, 3–29.

"Prima di tutto sono racconti" (First and Foremost, They Are Stories). *Sociologia del diritto* 1, 2004, 183–192.

"Fabbricare il tempo" (Making Time). *Sociologia del diritto* 1, 2003, 181–194.

Selected Book Chapters

"Davanti all'Altro. Ancora su diritto e pudore" (Before the Other: Further Reflections on Law and Modesty). In *ISLL Papers: The Online Collection of the Italian Society for Law and Literature*, Vol. 16, edited by C. Faralli and M. P. Mittica. 2023. Available online: https://doi.org/10.6092/unibo/amsacta/7188

"Nell'ordine del sentire. La forma giuridica come misura del vivente" (In the Order of Feeling: Legal Form as a Measure of the Living). In *La città dell'imperfezione. Follia e gioco tra Diritto e Letteratura*, edited by D. Cananzi, 49–62. Turin: Giappichelli, 2020.

"Narrare la dimensione umana per comprendere la dimensione giuridica" (Narrating the Human Dimension to Understand the Legal Dimension). In *Le arti e la dimensione giuridica*, edited by O. Roselli, 139–152. Bologna: Il Mulino, 2020.

"Fare della vita il mondo" (Making Life the World). In *Miti e narrazione della giustizia nel mondo greco*, edited by G. Forti and A. Provera, 231–240. Milan: Vita e Pensiero, 2019.

"Le radici letterarie antiche della dimensione giuridica europea" (The Ancient Literary Roots of the European Legal Dimension). In *Cultura giuridica e letteratura nella costruzione dell'Europa*, edited by O. Roselli, 89–102. Naples: Editoriale Scientifica, 2018.

"Aux origines du rapport entre droit et musique dans la Grèce antique" (On the Origins of the Relationship between Law and Music in Ancient Greece). In *Entre normes et sensibilitè: Droit et musique*, edited by P. Signorile, 35–45 Aix-en-Provence: PUAM, 2017.

"In-opera. Forme e alterità" (In-Opera: Forms and Otherness). In *Per una critica della giustizia: testi letterari e contesti storici a confronto*, edited by M.C. Foi, 152–159. Trieste: EUT, 2016.

"Diritto e letteratura. Disciplina, metodologia o movimento?" (Law and Literature: Discipline, Methodology or Movement?). In *Lingue e diritti*, Vol I. *Le parole della discriminazione. Diritto e letteratura*, edited by N. Maraschio, D. De Martino, and G. Stanchina, 111–138. Florence: Accademia della Crusca, 2014.

"Tra-Discipline" (In-Between Disciplines). In *Diritto, linguaggio e letteratura*, edited by R. Gualdo and R. Petrilli, 9–23. Perugia: Guerra Edizioni, 2013.

"Narrativas de mulheres a partir do mundo da vida" (Women's Narratives from the Lifeworld). In *Direito & Literatura: discurso, imaginário e normatividade*, edited by A.K. Trindade, R.M. Gubert, and A. Copetti, 307–343. Porto Alegre: Livraria do Advogado, 2010.

Index

 HTTPS://DOI.ORG/10.1163/9789004757714-010

www.ingramcontent.com/pod-product-compliance
Ingram Content Group UK Ltd.
Pitfield, Milton Keynes, MK11 3LW, UK
UKHW021031041026
15470UKWH00013B/1307

9 789004 757707